I0011849

MERN Café

LEARN MERN AS EASY AS SIPPING A COFFEE

PART 1 – MASTERING REACT BASICS & LAUNCHING MERN

Hari Narayn
Melbourne, VIC, Australia

ISBN: 9798324055271
Imprint: Independently published

Publisher: Amazon KDP
Author: Hari Narayn
Editor: Divya Raj
Cover idea by Hari Narayn
Cover image designed by DALL-E with minimal edits by Divya Raj

This book is dedicated to Ithal, the brightest joy and enduring happiness of my life. Your laughter lights up my world

Meet the Barista

 **Hari Narayn** is a seasoned techie with over 13 years of experience in designing and developing web and mobile applications. His expertise spans a range of technologies, including React, MERN, Microsoft 365, SharePoint, Azure, OpenAI, Teams, Power Platform, .Net, Angular, and JavaScript. Hari has delivered innovative web and mobile solutions for clients globally. He holds certifications as a Microsoft Certified Azure Solutions Architect Expert and a Microsoft Certified Azure AI Engineer. Additionally, Hari is the author of three technical books: two editions of 'Building the Modern Workplace with SharePoint Online' and 'Just React'. Originally from Kerala, India, he now resides in Melbourne, Victoria, Australia, where he works as a full stack engineer at Victoria Public Service.

Thanks a Latte

I am profoundly grateful to everyone who supported me during the creation of this book. Above all, I owe my deepest thanks to my family. To my wife, Divya, whose love, patience, and wisdom have been the cornerstone of my daily life, and to my daughter, Ithal, whose joy, and enthusiasm remind me of the wonder in our world—thank you both for your unwavering support and inspiration.

I also wish to express my gratitude to you, the readers of this book. Your interest and engagement are what bring this book to life, and for that, I am endlessly thankful.

I extend a heartfelt thank you to the readers of my previous work, "Just React." Your invaluable feedback has fueled my passion for writing, and I am truly grateful for your continued support and encouragement.

Finally, I deeply appreciate the continuous support from my publishing team at Amazon KDP, who believed in this project from the outset and played a crucial role in bringing it to fruition.

Café Menu: A Taste of What's Inside

First Sip

Welcome to MERN Café! This is the opening installment of our book series designed to guide you through crafting sophisticated web applications using the MERN stack—MongoDB, Express.js, React, and Node.js. This book is carefully blended to smooth your journey through the complex world of modern web development, presenting each concept like a well-steeped cup of coffee—rich in flavor yet easy to digest. Starting with the foundational beans and moving towards more refined brewing techniques, each chapter is crafted to layer upon the previous, ensuring a flavorful and enriching learning experience that deepens with every page.

The first four chapters are a deeper dive into the nuances of React, ensuring a solid understanding of its essential features. The last two chapters switch gears into the broader MERN landscape, blending a robust espresso into a full-bodied latte, integrating MongoDB, Express.js, and Node.js to create a full stack solution.

Chapter 1 sets the foundation by introducing React's core principles, including its declarative and component-based architecture that simplifies the creation of user interfaces. Here, we explore the Virtual DOM for optimized performance and JSX for its expressive power, preparing you for the intricate features of larger applications.

Chapter 2 guides you through configuring your development environment and assembling the basic building blocks of our application. This includes integrating TypeScript to enhance code stability and using React Router to ensure smooth component navigation, establishing a solid structural base for your application.

Chapter 3 delves into component communication within React, emphasizing the use of props for data transfer and the advantages of reusable components, with TypeScript ensuring strong type-checking. Chapter 4 expands on using React Context for efficient state management across the application, eliminating the need for prop drilling and facilitating easier data flows between components.

Chapter 5 bridges the gap between frontend and backend development by introducing full-stack techniques. Here, we connect React with MongoDB via Express.js, utilizing Node.js to orchestrate the server-side logic, effectively integrating all components of our MERN stack.

Chapter 6 completes the initial exploration by implementing a robust user authentication system, enhancing both the security and personalization of user experiences with Passport.js.

This book series is designed to not only make you proficient in handling individual technologies but also to give you the capability to integrate them effectively, creating applications that are both powerful and user-friendly. By the end, you will have developed a fully functional web application and acquired a basic understanding of React & MERN stack.

This is just the beginning of a journey that will prepare you to create cutting-edge applications that are not only functional but also a pleasure to interact with. Looking ahead, the rest of this book series will explore more advanced topics and features

We will introduce real-time functionalities, delve into microservices architecture for scalability, and tackle advanced MongoDB features. Additionally, we will explore more advanced React features.

Feel free to explore the final solution code of our project on our GitHub repository located at https://github.com/harinvp/merncafe. Additionally, you can access specific code sections for each chapter in the repository, mirroring those discussed in the book. This setup ensures convenient reference and accessibility throughout your reading journey. Could you have any questions about the content or code discussed in this book, please don't hesitate to create an issue in the repository. I am eager and ready to assist with any queries you may have.

So, enjoy the journey, one sip at a time!

CHAPTER 1

React Café

Cup

Welcome to the React Café – a revolutionary blend that has redefined the art of crafting web interfaces. In this chapter, we're starting on a journey to savor the essence of React and its distinct aroma compared to traditional JavaScript frameworks. We'll uncover why React has become the go-to choose for developers worldwide, revealing its unique recipe for crafting dynamic and efficient user interfaces. From the concept of the Virtual DOM to the robust flavors of components, state management, and the aromatic JSX syntax, we'll sip and relish the key ingredients that make React a true game-changer in modern web development. So, grab your favorite cup of coffee and let's indulge in the delightful world of React!

React, The Ideal Roast

1) Components Galore: React's foundation in components is like assembling Lego blocks, offering unparalleled flexibility and ease of maintenance in application development. It's the ultimate Lego playground for developers.

2) Virtual DOM Magic: Imagine having a clone of your work that you can tweak endlessly without disturbing the original. That's Virtual DOM for you – it ensures seamless updates without disrupting user experience. It's like making edits on the fly without missing a beat!

3) JSX Fusion: With JSX, blending HTML and JavaScript becomes a breeze. Building UI elements feels like a seamless dance between the two, resulting in cleaner and more expressive code.

4) One-Way Street: React's one-way data flow simplifies development by ensuring that data moves in a consistent, unidirectional manner. No more back-and-forth struggles – just smooth sailing like a serene river.

5) Simplicity in State: React's approach to state management is both straightforward and effective, making it a joy for developers to handle. It's simplicity at its finest.

6) Blazing Performance: Thanks to its efficient architecture and streamlined processes, React delivers top-notch performance even in the most complex applications. It's like watching a Ferrari zoom past – smooth, swift, and exhilarating!

7) Community Love: The vibrant React community offers a treasure trove of support, tools, and libraries to cater to every developer's needs. It's like having an army of allies ready to lend a hand whenever you need it.

The Virtual DOM - Brewing Brilliance

Let's look at how React's efficiency and performance compared to pure JS. Consider our upcoming website, where various items will be showcased. Customers can add items to their cart. Let's delve into how both React, and plain JavaScript manage this functionality.

Look at the below JavaScript code. Refer to Code 1.1.

```
Code 1.1 - eApp.html
<!-- HTML -->
<div id="app">
  <h1>John & Mila (Pure JS)</h1>
  <div>
    <button onclick="addToCart()">Add Polo to
cart</button>
  </div>
  <br />
```

The JavaScript part contains the functionality of adding a polo shirt to the cart. Initially, there are variables poloCount (count of polos in the cart), price (total price), and cart (array to store polo shirt details, although it's not used here).

The addToCart() function is triggered when the button is clicked. It updates the poloCount and and the price. Then, it updates the text content of elements with IDs liPoloCount and liPrice to display the updated counts and price on the webpage.

This code simulates a basic online store where you can add polo shirts to your cart, and it dynamically updates the displayed count and total price whenever you add a polo to the cart.

Imagine how it will be represented as a Document Object Model (DOM) tree. We have a div at the top of the tree. The elements h1, div, ul and the button are the child elements.

The function addToCart, accesses the polo count menu item first, using its id. So, here JS traverses the DOM tree and access the menu item element (li). Next it does the same thing for the price menu item.

Let's see this action in the browser. Save the file as eApp.html, and open it in the browser. Then click on F12 to open developer tools. Refer to image 1.1.

John & Mila (Vanilla JS)

Image 1.1 E-cart html with dev tools

As illustrated in Image 1.1, inspect the HTML elements within the DevTools' Elements tab. Whenever you click on Add Polo, it triggers updates to the li elements representing both the count and price, in the DOM.

This means, every time an item is added to the cart, two DOM updates occur: one for updating the count and another for updating the price. If you add 20 items to the cart, this results in a total of 40 DOM updates, as each addition triggers both count and price updates. This means that even for adding the same item multiple times, each addition leads to two DOM updates.

You may wonder whether the browser repaints the entire page with each DOM change. It's important to note that modern browsers have evolved to optimize rendering processes. When changes are made to the DOM, the entire page doesn't necessarily need to be repainted. Instead, browsers are now adept at identifying and updating only the specific parts of the DOM that have been modified. In other words, only the elements that have undergone changes are re-rendered, minimizing unnecessary repaints and optimizing performance. Therefore, in our scenario, the concern with this plain JS code is on the frequency of updates to the DOM and not about repeated repainting of the entire page.

Let's explore how React handles the given scenario compared to plain JavaScript. To do this, you can use CodeSandbox.io to create a React sandbox. By navigating to www.codesandbox.io and following the prompts, we can set up a React sandbox. It's recommended to create a login to easily refer to the project later. Once inside the CodeSandbox environment, you'll locate the App.js file Refer to Image 1.2.

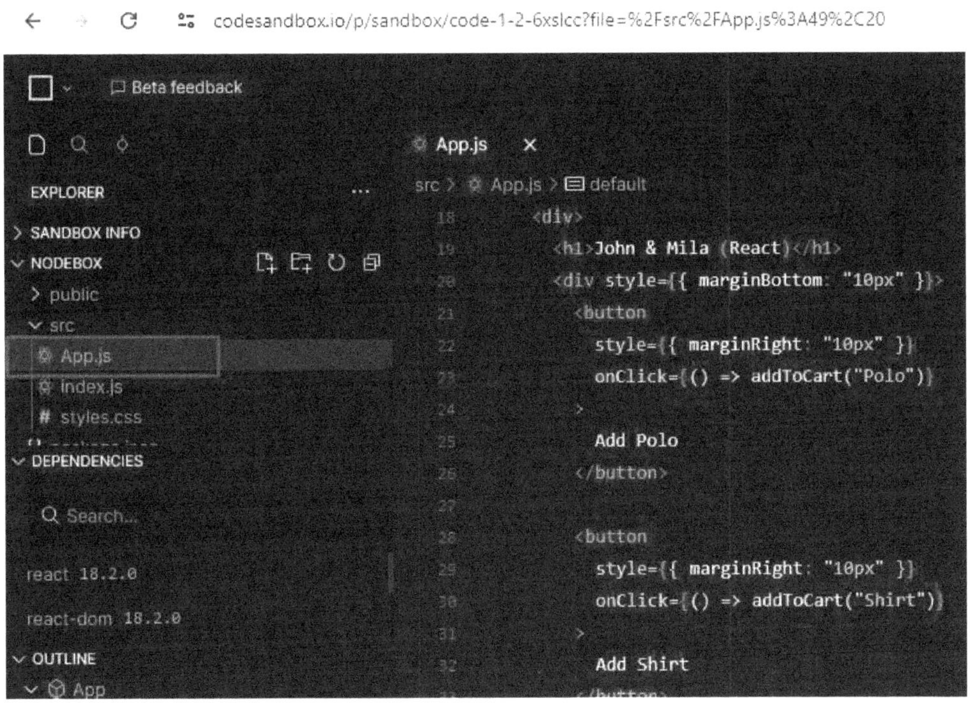

Image 1.2 - CodeSandbox

Replace the App.js with the below code outlined in Code 1-2.

Code 1.2 - eApp.jsx

```
import React, { useState } from "react";

function App() {
  const [poloCount, setPoloCount] = useState(0);
  const [price, setPrice] = useState(0);
  const addToCart = () => {
    setPoloCount(poloCount + 1);
    setPrice(price + 10);
  };
```

```
return (
    <div>
      <h1>John & Mila (React)</h1>
      <div style={{ marginBottom: "10px" }}>
        <button onClick={addToCart}>Add Polo to
cart</button>
      </div>
      <ul>
        <li>{`${poloCount} Polos`}</li>
        <li>{`${price} AUD`}</li>
      </ul>
    </div>
  );
}
export default App;
```

Don't worry about the complexities of the code at this moment. It will become clear as you learn more about the concepts later. For now, simply observe how this code behaves when executed on CodeSandbox. You'll notice that it performs the same function as the pure JavaScript code.

When you click the Add Polo to cart button, React handles things differently compared to plain JavaScript. It keeps track of the count and price changes internally as part of its "state".

React uses something called a "Virtual DOM" to manage these changes. This means that when you use functions like useState in React to update the state, React batches these updates together instead of applying them one by one directly to the real DOM.

So, even though there may be multiple changes happening (like adding 20 products to the cart), React smartly groups them together and applies them all at once to the actual webpage. This means that instead of making 40 individual updates to the DOM as in plain JavaScript, React efficiently applies all the changes in just one go. This optimized approach reduces unnecessary work for the browser, making the webpage more efficient and responsive.

Execute the code in sandbox and interact with it to see how the DOM changes applied at one shot. You can use preview console button on the right and switch to Elements tab to see how the DOM changes got applied at once. Refer to image 1.3 where steps are highlighted.

`Image 1.3 – Batching of DOM changes in React

This is the result of React's Virtual DOM feature, which is a smart mechanism that groups DOM changes together. It utilizes state management to achieve this optimization.

There's a common misunderstanding about the Virtual DOM, assuming it's solely about selectively reloading parts of the DOM as needed. However, plain JavaScript also allows for loading only specific parts of the DOM. What sets React's Virtual DOM apart is its ability to batch these partial changes and apply them to the actual DOM all at once. You've observed this firsthand by inspecting the browser's developer tools.

Stateful Components: Crafting the Foundation of React

Now let's go through the above piece of React code we created earlier and let me explain about Components, state & JSX. Refer to Code 1.2.

In the React code we've written, we have what's called a "functional component" named App. Think of this component like a special tool that helps us create a specific part of our website – in this case, a shopping cart.

Now, this shopping cart needs to keep track of a couple of things: how many polo shirts the customer wants to buy (we call this poloCount), and the total price of all the polos in the cart (we call this price).

To manage these pieces of information, we use something called state. It's like a memory bank where our components can store and remember important details. In our code, we're using a special tool called useState hook to create and manage this state. It's a bit like having a notebook where we jot down the number of polos and their prices.

So, whenever someone clicks the button to add a polo to their cart, our component knows to update the number of polos and the total price, and it does this by referring to the information stored in its state. This way, our shopping cart always stays up to date with the latest counts and prices.

The App component is a building block of your application that manages its own state and defines the structure and behavior of a part of the user interface. Components like these can be reused, combined, and composed to create more complex UIs in a modular and maintainable way.

Let's compare the concept of state to something we can relate to in real life, like a cooler in your room. Imagine the cooler as a component in your room, responsible for managing and showing both the current room temperature and the desired cooler temperature. Think of your room as the React app.

Now, the state of this cooler unit has two parts:
1. Room Temperature: This is the current temperature in your room, which can change based on different factors.

2. Cooler Setting: This is the temperature set on the cooler to make your room cooler. You can adjust this setting to make yourself more comfortable. Let's say we've set it to 20 degrees Celsius for now.
For instance, if you're feeling too warm, you might adjust the cooler setting to lower the temperature. Changing this setting causes a change in the state of the cooler unit. When you lower the temperature dial, the cooler works harder to cool the room. So, the cooler temperature is a state of the component that you can change. This change in state eventually updates both the desired temperature and, consequently, the room temperature.

Just like the cooler unit continually displays both the current room temperature and the cooler setting, a React component keeps rendering and displaying its current state. As the room temperature changes or the cooler setting is adjusted (changes its state), the display on the cooler unit updates to show the new values.

Users interact with the room cooler unit by using a remote to adjust the cooler setting to achieve a comfortable room temperature. Similarly, in a React component, users interact by clicking buttons or using controls to adjust settings that cause changes in the component's state.

So, in this analogy, the room cooler unit represents a React component, with the room temperature and cooler setting representing its state. Adjusting the cooler setting is like updating the state in a React component. The continuous display of both the room temperature and cooler setting corresponds to rendering in React, reflecting the current state of the component.

In your room, just as you have various items serving specific or multiple functions, a React app consists of multiple components. Let's consider the example of a desk. Think of having a desk in your room. Sometimes, it serves as your dedicated workspace, where you organize notes and work on projects. At other times, it transforms into a dining table, where you gather with friends and family to enjoy meals. In this scenario, the desk serves as a reusable component, adapting to different purposes based on your needs. Similarly, in a React app, components can be reused across various parts of the application, just like how the desk serves different functions in your room.

(Just remember, if it's a standing desk, refrain from accidentally lifting it up during dinner – that could lead to quite the unexpected mealtime experience!)

Discovering the Essence: Rendering with JSX

Let's delve into the concept of rendering, which is fundamental to how elements are displayed in React.

In our code example (Code 1.2), if we examine the return statement, we can observe that the component is responsible for rendering a title, a button, and a list that showcases the number of polo shirts in the cart (`poloCount`) and the total price (`price`). This mirrors the functionality of a cooler, which typically displays both the temperature setting and the current room temperature.

Consider the digital display on a cooler, which presents information in a clear and specific format. Similarly, in React, JSX – JavaScript XML – is used to define the structure and appearance of UI elements. JSX is a special syntax that allows us to write HTML-like code directly inside JavaScript. JSX serves as a powerful tool that enables developers to express UI code in a manner that closely resembles HTML, thus enhancing readability and expressiveness.

JSX acts as a syntax extension for JavaScript, providing developers with a concise and intuitive way to describe the composition of components. It allows for the seamless integration of JavaScript logic with HTML-like syntax, facilitating the creation of dynamic and interactive user interfaces.

It's important to understand that while JSX shares similarities with HTML, it ultimately undergoes transformation into JavaScript before being rendered by the browser. This transformation process enables React to efficiently manage and manipulate the DOM, resulting in a smooth and responsive user experience.

Sip

In this chapter, we explored the fundamental concepts that make React a powerful and distinctive tool for building modern web applications. We began by discussing the motivations behind using React and how it addresses common challenges faced by developers. Unlike traditional JavaScript frameworks, React introduces a declarative and component-based approach to building user interfaces, which offers greater flexibility, reusability, and maintainability.

One of the key innovations introduced by React is the concept of the Virtual DOM. By maintaining a lightweight representation of the actual DOM in memory, React optimizes rendering performance by minimizing unnecessary updates and efficiently diffing changes. This enables React to deliver fast and responsive user experiences, even for complex applications.

React's architecture is all about components, which encapsulate discrete units of UI functionality. Components promote modularity and code reuse, allowing developers to compose rich user interfaces from smaller, self-contained building blocks. Additionally, React components can manage their own internal state, enabling dynamic and interactive user experiences.

We also discussed JSX, a syntax extension for JavaScript that allows developers to define the structure and appearance of UI elements in a familiar and expressive manner. JSX seamlessly integrates HTML-like syntax within JavaScript code, facilitating the creation of intuitive and readable UI components.

Let's Begin Brewing in the next chapter by creating a React Project and start tasting the Experience.

CHAPTER 2

Brewing React

Cup

Welcome to the next step of our React learning! In this chapter, we'll be diving deep into the foundational aspects of React development, covering everything from setting up our development environment to designing and structuring our application using components.
We'll start by firing up the essential tools, including Visual Studio Code and npm, and walk through the process of creating a new React project using create-react-app. With our project in place, we'll take a closer look at the key files and folders within a React project, touching on the basics of TypeScript along the way.

Once we've familiarized ourselves with the project structure, we'll shift our focus to the heart of React development: components. We'll learn how to design and create major components, including our central App component, and assemble our app's Navigation system for seamless navigation between different parts of our application.

Along the way, we'll delve into the fundamentals of routing, explore UI design principles, and discover the power of CSS modules for maintaining clean and modular styles. By the end of this chapter, you'll not only have a firm grasp of the essential tools required for React development but also a foundational understanding of component design. You'll learn how to create and develop basic components, setting the stage for more React concepts in the chapters ahead.

Crafting the Perfect Blend of Tools

Let's get started by setting up our favorite Integrated Development Environment (IDE), Visual Studio Code. You can download the latest version from this link: https://code.visualstudio.com. Once you've got Visual Studio Code installed, the next step is to download Node Version Manager (NVM) from this link: https://github.com/coreybutler/nvm-windows/releases/download/1.1.12/nvm-setup.exe .

Node.js is like the engine that powers React development. It's a software platform that allows us to run JavaScript code outside of a web browser, directly on our computer. This means we can build, and test React applications on our own machines before deploying them to the web.

Node.js also comes with a package manager called npm. Think of npm like a big online store where we can find and download all sorts of useful tools and libraries to help us build our React projects more easily. These tools can range from simple utilities to complex frameworks that handle things like routing, state management, and more.

Now, NVM (Node Version Manager) is a handy tool that helps us manage different versions of Node.js on our computer. This is important because different projects may require different versions of Node.js to run properly. With NVM, we can easily switch between these versions as needed without having to uninstall and reinstall Node.js each time.

So, in summary, Node.js provides the foundation for React development by giving us the runtime environment and tools we need to build and test our applications. And NVM helps us manage different versions of Node.js so we can work on multiple projects without any compatibility issues.

Now that you've installed both Visual Studio Code and NVM, open Visual Studio Code. You'll notice a terminal at the bottom. Navigate to your desired folder in the terminal.

Next, let's install the latest version of Node.js. Run the following command:
```
nvm install -ts
```

This command will install the latest available version of Node.js. To see the version that's been installed, run:

```
nvm ls
```

Once you've identified the version installed, use the following command to switch to it:
```
nvm use 20.11.0
```

Replace "20.11.0" with the version that's installed on your machine.

Now, let's install Create React App globally. From your Visual Studio Code terminal, run:
```
npm install -g create-react-app
```

This command installs Create React App, a tool that helps us quickly set up new React projects.

Create React App is like a magical tool that makes it super easy for people to start building websites or applications using React. It sets up everything you need to write, test, and run your React code without you having to worry about the complex setup details.

Imagine you want to make a delicious sandwich. You could go to the store, buy all the ingredients, prep the vegetables, cook the meat, and assemble it all from scratch. It's a lot of work, and you need to know how to do each step.

Create React App – it's like a pre-packaged sandwich-making kit you can buy. This kit comes with everything you need to make a tasty sandwich without worrying about the detailed process. It includes fresh ingredients, pre-cooked meat, sauces, and even the bread. All neatly organized and ready for you.

With Create React App, it's like having a sandwich kit where you just need to "heat it and go." The kit sets up a similar kind of "heat it and go" convenience for building a web application with React. It provides you with the necessary tools, configurations, and a good starting point, so you can focus on creating your React app without getting bogged down by the complexities of setting up the development environment.

You're all set up and ready to start building with React.

Starting Your React Brew

Let's kick off by creating our React app using the command:

```
npx create-react-app milajo-ecommerce --template
typescript
```

This command will generate a new React app named `milajo-ecommerce` with TypeScript configuration already set up. If you encounter an execution policy error, you can bypass it for the session using the following command: `Set-ExecutionPolicy -Scope Process -ExecutionPolicy Bypass`

After running the command, navigate to the newly created 'milajo-ecommerce' folder using:
```
cd milajo-ecommerce
```

Next, open the folder in Visual Studio Code by selecting File -> Open Folder and choosing the `milajo-ecommerce` folder. You may be prompted to `Trust the authors`, so go ahead and do so.

When you create a React app using `create-react-app`, it generates various files and folders to help organize and set up your project. Specifically, by using the `--template typescript` option, we instruct Create React App to scaffold the project with TypeScript configuration and setup already in place.

Why do we use TypeScript for our project? In JavaScript, variables can hold values of any type, and there's no compile-time checking to ensure that variables are used in a type-safe manner. This can lead to runtime errors that are difficult to debug, especially in larger codebases. TypeScript catches type-related errors during development, before the code is executed, reducing the chances of runtime errors in production.

Let's go through the important folders/files in our created project.

1) `public` folder:
   - `index.html`: This is the main HTML file that represents your app. It contains a `<div>` element with an `id` of `root` where your React app will be rendered.

2) `src` folder:

- `index.tsx`: This is the entry point of your React app. It's where React gets started and renders your app into the HTML document.
- `App.tsx` This is often the main component of your app. It defines how your app looks and behaves. You can create additional components and import them into `App.tsx` as needed.
- `App.css`: This is the stylesheet for styling your component/s.

3) `node_modules` folder:

The `node_modules` folder is like a box that holds all the tools and resources your app needs to work correctly. It's filled with various files and folders that contain different pieces of code, called dependencies or libraries.

When you create a new React app or install additional features, npm (Node Package Manager) automatically adds the necessary dependencies to this folder. You don't need to worry about what's inside or how it works; npm takes care of all the behind-the-scenes work for you.

Think of the node_modules folder as your app's pantry, stocked with all the ingredients it needs to cook up a successful project. If everything is in there, your app should run smoothly!

4) package.json:

The package.json file is like a blueprint or a recipe card for your project. It contains important information about your project, such as its name, version number, and a list of all the ingredients it needs to work correctly. These ingredients are called dependencies and devDependencies and are listed with their version numbers.

In addition to listing dependencies, the package.json file also includes scripts. These scripts are like step-by-step instructions for performing various tasks related to your project, such as starting the development server, building the production version of your app, or running tests.

The package.json file is like the master plan for your project. It tells you what your project is made of and how to perform common tasks associated with it. Whenever you need to add a new dependency or run a script, you can refer to this file to see what's already there and what needs to be done.

5) tsconfig.json: The tsconfig.json file is like a set of instructions that TypeScript follows when it's turning your TypeScript code into regular JavaScript code that the browser can understand. It contains different settings and configurations that tell TypeScript how to handle things like which version of JavaScript to output, how to deal with errors, and where to find additional files.

You can think of the `tsconfig.json` file as a control panel for TypeScript. It allows you to customize how TypeScript behaves for your specific project needs. For example, you can specify whether you want to target newer versions of JavaScript, how strict you want the compiler to be, and where to find additional files or libraries.

By editing the `tsconfig.json` file, you can tailor TypeScript's behavior to fit your project perfectly. It's like fine-tuning a recipe to get the exact flavor you're looking for.

As you dive into your project, your focus will be on the files located within the `src` folder. These files, like `App.tsx`, serve as the foundation for building your application's components and adding functionality. The `.tsx` extension indicates that these files are written in TypeScript and contain JSX syntax, which is essential for creating dynamic user interfaces and interactive components. So, whenever you're working on enhancing your application, these are the files you'll be tinkering with the most.

Let's see the App in browser. Click View->Terminal and run `npm run start`. This will launch your default web browser and open a new tab with the address http://localhost:3000 . From there, you'll be able to view your React application. You can refer to Image 1.5 and 1.6 for visuals of how my VS Code editor and the web browser appear at this stage.

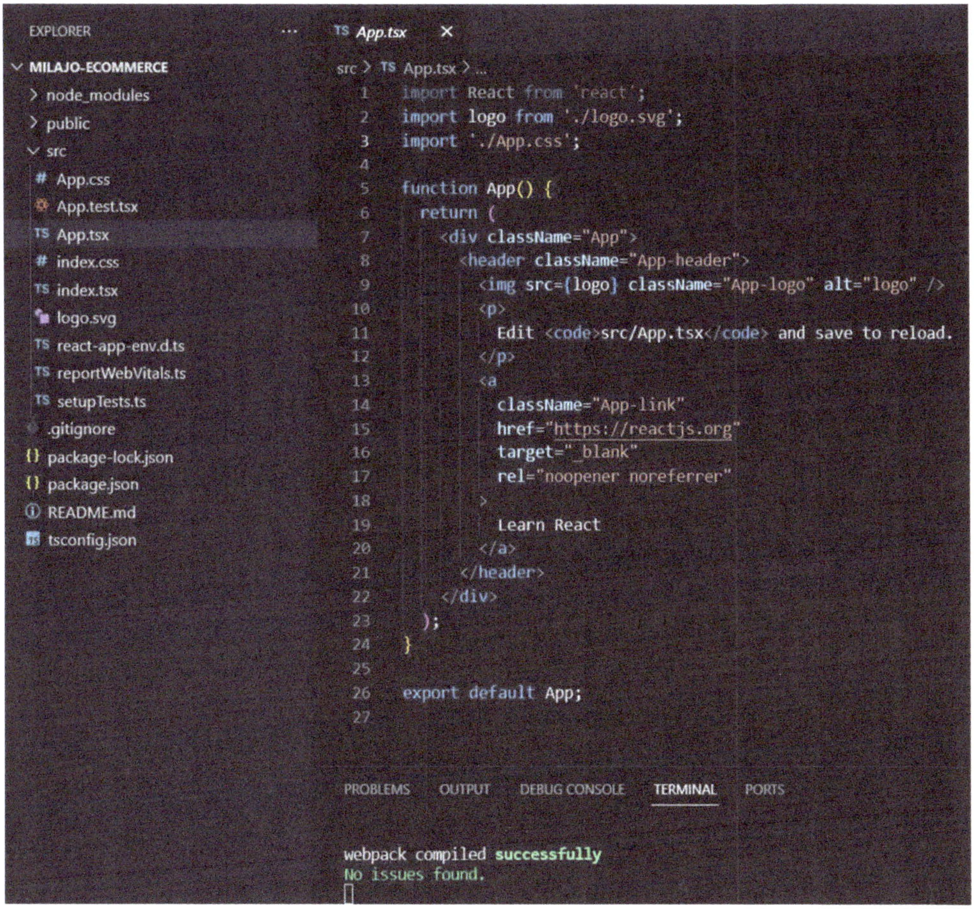

Image 2.1 – React Project VS Code Editor

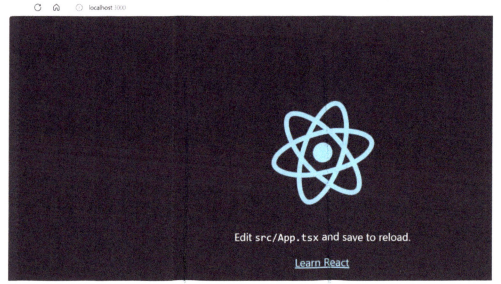

Edit src/App.tsx and save to reload.

Learn React

Image 2.2 – App in browser

Component Design

Now, let's sketch out the blueprint for a basic e-commerce application using React. In this initial part of the book, our focus is on creating a simplified example to illustrate fundamental React concepts. We'll gradually introduce more complexity and additional features in the subsequent part of this series.

Let's summarize the requirements for this phase:

Users will be able to browse a selection of products on the home page. Each product will include a picture, a title, a description, and a price. Users can click on a button to add a product to their shopping cart, and they can add as many products as they like.

Once users have finished shopping, they can review their shopping cart. It will display all the products they've added along with the total price. From there, users can choose to proceed to checkout and purchase the products.

After completing a purchase, users will have access to their order history on the My Order page. This page will show all the orders with their status.

So, let's determine what are the major components we needed to build this:

App Component (App.tsx):
- The main component that renders the entire application.
- Manages the overall structure, layout, and navigation of the app.
- Includes routing to switch between different views or pages.

Catalog (Home) Component (Catalog.tsx):
- Displays a list of products available for purchase.
- Handles the rendering of individual Item components.
- Serves as the Home page of the App

Item Component (Item.tsx):
- Represents a single product in the list.
- Displays basic product information like name and price.
- Includes an "Add to Cart" button.

Trolley Component (Trolley.tsx):
- Displays the items added to the shopping cart.
- Shows product names, quantities, and their price.
- Calculates and displays the total cost.
- Place Order button and message.

My Orders Component (MyOrders.tsx):
- Display orders with the status.

That's all for now! Let's start writing the code.

We already have a default App component. Create three more components.
Right click on *src* folder and click *New Folder*. Name it as *components*.
Now right click on *components* folder, and click *New File*. Name it as
Catalog.tsx. Add the following code into that. Refer to Code 2.1.

```
Code 2.1: Catalog component - base
function Catalog() {
  return (
    <div>Catalog</div>
  );
}
export default Catalog;
```

Let me explain this code. This code defines a component called Catalog. Think
of a component as a small piece of a webpage. In this case, the Catalog
component creates a box with the word "Catalog" inside it.

Inside the `function Catalog()`, you'll see JSX.. So when we write
`<div>Catalog</div>`, it's like saying, `Create a box (a <div>) with`
`the word Catalog inside it.`

When we write `export default Catalog`, it means we're making this
component available for other parts of our website to use. So, whenever we
need a Catalog component in another component, we can easily add it.

So, this code serves as a foundation for our component. Later, we'll make
modifications to turn it into our catalog. Now, let's create three more files
under *components* folder: `Item.tsx`, `Trolley.tsx` and `MyOrders.tsx`.
In these files, we'll start with similar code structures. You can refer to Code
2.2 for Item, Code 2.3 for Trolley, and Code 2.4 for My Orders.

Code 2.2: Item component - base

```
function Item() {
  return (
    <div>Item</div>
  );
}
export default Item;
```

Code 2.3: Trolley component - base

```
function Trolley() {
  return (
    <div>Trolley</div>
  );
}
export default Trolley;
```

Code 2.4: My Orders component - base

```
function MyOrders() {
  return (
    <div>My Orders</div>
  );
}
export default MyOrders;
```

App Component

Let's start on designing the App component. By the end of this process, you'll gain knowledge in the following key concepts in React:

1) Import: This involves bringing in external modules or components into our project to use in our code.

2) Routing: Routing is like creating a roadmap for our application, determining which components to display based on the current URL or location.

3) Using Material UI for UI design: Material UI is a popular library that provides pre-designed components and styles to enhance the visual appearance of our app.
4) Using CSS Modules for styling: CSS Modules allow us to scope our CSS styles to individual components, preventing style conflicts and making our code more modular and maintainable.

To install npm packages, terminate the current run in the terminal, press Ctrl+C. This will stop the execution of the current process and return you to the terminal.

Let's dive into each of these concepts and see how they come together to craft our App component.

1) Setting up navigation & adding a header:

To set up navigation, we'll use `react-router-dom` library. Think of navigation as creating pathways for users to move between different parts of our app, like switching between pages.

To install `react-router-dom`, run a command in our terminal: npm `install react-router-dom`. This library provides us with tools to handle navigation in our React app.

Now, let's add a header that will appear on every page of our app. To do this, we'll use another library called Material-UI (MUI). It's like getting a pre-made design kit for our app, so we don't have to start from scratch.

We can install Material-UI by running the following command in our terminal: npm `install @mui/material @mui/icons-material @emotion/react @emotion/styled @mui/styled-engine @mui/icons-material`.This command installs Material-UI as a dependency for our project, giving us access to a wide range of pre-designed components and icons to use in our app.

Copy the following code (Code 2.5) into App.`tsx`, to set up the navigation and header. . I'll provide detailed explanations for each part below.

```
Code 2.5: App Component
// Importing necessary tools from the react toolbox
import { BrowserRouter as Router, Routes, Route, NavLink }
from 'react-router-dom';

// Importing MUI components for the header UI
import { AppBar, Toolbar, Typography, Container,
IconButton } from '@mui/material';
```

```jsx
import StoreTwoToneIcon from '@mui/icons-
material/StoreTwoTone';
// Importing custom components (Catalog, Item, Trolley)
import Catalog from './components/Catalog';
import Trolley from './components /Trolley';
import MyOrders from '. /components/MyOrders';

function App() {
  return (
    <Router>
      <div>
        {/* Material-UI AppBar for the header */}
        <AppBar position="static">
          <Toolbar>
            {/* Logo using the MUI Store icon */}
            <StoreTwoToneIcon fontSize="large"
sx={{paddingRight:"10px"}}/>
              {/* App name */}
            <Typography variant="h6" component="div" sx={{
flexGrow: 1 }}>
              MilaJo
            </Typography>

            {/* Navigation links */}
            <NavLink to="/ " style={{ color: 'inherit',
textDecoration: 'none', marginRight: '20px' }}>
              Home

 </ NavLink >
            <NavLink to="/trolley" style={{ color:
'inherit', textDecoration: 'none', marginRight: '20px' }}>
              Trolley
            </NavLink >
```

```
            <NavLink to="/myorders " style={{ color:
'inherit', textDecoration: 'none' }}>
                My Orders
            </NavLink >
          </Toolbar>
        </AppBar>
        {/* Defining routes and specifying which
components to render for each route */}
        <Container>
          <Routes>
            <Route path="/ " element={<Catalog />} />
            <Route path="/trolley" element={<Trolley />}
/>
            <Route path="/myorders" element={<MyOrders />}
/>
          </Routes>
        </Container>
      </div>
    </Router>
  );
}
// Making the App function available for other parts of
the application
export default App;
```

1) Imports:

Think of import as a way for our React app to borrow tools or features from a special toolbox (in this case, a package like react-router-dom).

`import { BrowserRouter as Router, Routes, Route, Link }` `from 'react-router-dom';` This line imports specific tools from the `react-router-dom` library, such as the `BrowserRouter` for setting up navigation, `Routes` for defining routes, `Route` for specifying individual routes, and `NavLink` for creating clickable links.

The following two import statements import components and icons from Material-UI to our React component. `AppBar` provides a consistent navigation header at the top of your application, typically used for branding and navigation links.

The `Toolbar` usually goes inside an `AppBar` and holds other components like buttons, icons, or additional navigation elements. The `Typography` is used for displaying text with customizable styles and variants, such as headings, paragraphs, or captions.

The `Container` provides a fixed-width container for your content, ensuring consistent spacing and layout across different screen sizes. `StoreTwoToneIcon` is a specific icon representing a store, with a two-tone design, suitable for use in our e-commerce context.

The remaining three imports are for importing our own custom components. So, when you import Catalog means, you want to use the code in that component in the App component.

2) Return Statement (JSX):

The return statement contains JSX code, which represents the structure and content of the component.
`<AppBar>`: The Material-UI app bar represents our app header with a toolbar containing a logo and an app name. The logo is represented by an icon button with the Store icon, and the app name is displayed as text within the app bar.

`<Router>`: This sets up the router, allowing the application to handle navigation based on the URL.

`<div>`: A container for the entire content of the app.

`<NavLink>`: Used to create navigation elements within the app without triggering a full page refresh.

`<Routes>`: This is where you define the routes and specify which components to render for each route.

3) Routes:

`<Route path="/ " element={<Catalog />} />`: This says, When the URL is /, render the Catalog component. Similar case for Trolley and MyOrders routes. For `Trolley` component, the URL is `/trolley`.

Once you run the app using the command `npm run start` in the terminal, you'll notice that a navigation system is already set up. Clicking on links within the app will display different components without causing a full-page refresh. Currently, we only have placeholder content, so clicking on links will simply display that content.

By default, the App opens the Catalog page as we had set Home link route to Catalog page. When you click on My Orders, You will have notice that the browser URL is pointing to `/myorders`. That means we are on the My Orders page. Remember, Currently, the `MyOrders` component only contains placeholder content, which is being displayed as My orders. The content indicates that we are in the `MyOrders` component.

You can see an example of this navigation in action in Image 2.3, where I navigated to the My Orders component. The browser route and the selected menu are highlighted.

Image 2.3 App Navigation

You might have noticed that even though we're on the My Orders page, the My Orders menu item isn't highlighted in the navigation bar. We can fix this using a special feature of NavLink, that allows us to apply a specific style to the link when it matches the current URL. This is achieved using the isActive property, which allows you to define CSS classes or inline styles that are applied to the link when it is active.

Instead of using inline styles, we'll use a basic CSS module for the App component and achieve this part.

CSS modules are a way to organize CSS stylesheets by scoping them to individual components. When you rename a CSS file with the module.css extension, build tools recognize it as a CSS module. This means that the styles defined in that file will only apply to the component they're imported into, preventing them from affecting other parts of the application. CSS modules help keep styles modular and maintainable, especially in larger projects where conflicts between styles can occur.

Rename App.css to App.module.css. By naming CSS files with the module.css extension, build tools recognize them as CSS modules and apply specific transformations during the build process.

Now add the replace the code in App.module.css with the below code. Refer to Code 2.6:

```
Code 2.6: App.module.css
.menuLink {
  color: inherit;

 text-decoration: none;
  margin-right: 20px;
}
.activeLink {
  background-color: #FF5733;
  border-radius: 10%;
  padding: 10px 10px 10px 10px;
}
```

.menuLink class is defined for styling regular menu items, while .activeLink is used for styling the active menu item, giving it a distinctive background color, rounded corners, and padding to visually highlight it.

Now, let's modify the App.tsx to include this styling by using the isActive property of NavLink.

First, import the CSS module using the below line. Add this line to the imports section.
```
import appStyles from "./App.module.css";
```

when you `import App.module.css` using the above line, you're essentially importing an object (`appStyles`) that contains mappings from the class names defined in `App.module.css` to unique identifiers generated by the build tool. This allows you to access and use the CSS class names in your component while ensuring their scoping and avoiding naming conflicts.

Next, replace the `NavLink` section in `App.tsx` with the below code. Refer to Code 2.7.

Code 2.7: App.tsx - NavLink updates
```
  {/* Navigation links */}
<NavLink className={({ isActive }) =>
  `${appStyles.menuLink} ${isActive ? appStyles.activeLink
: ""}`
} to="/catalog" >
  Home
</NavLink>
<NavLink className={({ isActive }) =>
  `${appStyles.menuLink} ${isActive ? appStyles.activeLink
: ""}`
} to="/trolley">
  Trolley
</NavLink>
<NavLink className={({ isActive }) =>
  `${appStyles.menuLink} ${isActive ? appStyles.activeLink
: ""}`
} to="/myorders" >
  My Orders
</NavLink>
```

Here, we removed inline styles and added a `className` property, to all the four links.

```
className={(({ isActive }) =>`${appStyles.menuLink}
${isActive ? appStyles.activeLink : ""}`
```

This line of code dynamically assigns CSS class names to an element's className attribute based on a condition.

When user clicks on a particular menu item, the corresponding link is routed to a new page or component within the application. When this routing occurs, the NavLink component responsible for the menu item, receives a special isActive prop provided by the react-router-dom library.

The isActive prop is automatically set to true when the link's destination matches the current URL of the application. This means that when the user navigates to the page or component associated with the clicked menu item, the corresponding NavLink or Link component will receive the isActive prop as true.

Now, save the changes and you can see in the browser that the selected menu item gets highlighted. Refer to Image 2.4.

Image 2.4 App Navigation with highlighted selection

Sip

In this chapter, we started our journey into React development by establishing our development environment using VS Code, Node.js and npm. We initiated our project with create-react-app and familiarized ourselves with the structure of a typical React project, examining key files and directories. Additionally, we introduced TypeScript, a powerful tool for adding static typing to JavaScript, enhancing the robustness and maintainability of our codebase.

Transitioning to the design phase of our application, we constructed the foundational App component and explored fundamental UI design principles. We implemented a navigation bar to facilitate smooth navigation between different components, leveraging React Router for efficient routing within our application. Through this process, we gained insights into the significance of routing in creating a cohesive user experience.

Furthermore, we delved into the importance of CSS modules for organizing and managing component-specific styles, ensuring maintainability, and preventing style conflicts. Additionally, we learned how to import components into one another, fostering modularity and code reuse within our application.

Looking ahead to the next chapter, we will deepen our understanding of React by building the catalog for our e-commerce site. This will involve a detailed exploration of Props and State, foundational concepts in React that enable the creation of dynamic and interactive components.

Talking Components

Cup

In this chapter, let's continue the delightful journey through our React Café, where our focus will be on props and component communication. We'll explore how different parts of our React application interact and exchange information to create a fluid user experience. In the process, we will brew up some essential components for our e-commerce application.

We will start by setting up the image mapping by carefully selecting the finest coffee beans, ensuring each image is perfectly showcased. Next, we'll craft the Item component, where each product detail is carefully blended - title, description, and price. Along the way, we'll savor the rich flavors of React's features: functional components, where each sip brings simplicity and clarity; props, serving as our guiding recipe for passing data from parent to child components; and the concept of reusability, much like enjoying your favorite coffee blend again and again.

As we explore these components, we'll also sprinkle in some TypeScript magic, ensuring our ingredients are precisely measured and our components are brewed to perfection. So, grab your favorite cup, and let's brew the Catalog component in our cozy café!

Crafting Catalog

Let's break down the process of building the catalog into three simple steps:

1) Setting up Image Mapping: We'll start by arranging different images for our products using an Image Mapper. This step involves creating a visual map of images, especially tailored for each product.

2) Building the Item Component: Next, we'll construct the Item component, which showcases an individual product and provides options for adding it to the shopping cart.

3) Constructing the Catalog Component: In the final step, we'll assemble the Catalog component, which serves as a platform for hosting multiple items together in a cohesive manner.

Image Mapping

We'll kick off with Step 1. By the end of this phase, you'll grasp the concept of props in React.

To begin, download the images from our GitHub repository https://github.com/harinvp/merncafe The images are located under milajo-ecommerce -> client -> src-> images.

These 10 images are categorized into four types: 3 handbags, 3 watches, 3 shoes, and one ring. These images are gathered from unsplash.com. All the used images we use are free to use and in addition, we will properly attribute each.

Copy the images to a designated folder within our React application directory. Let's create an images folder under the src folder and save all the images there.
Note that for this initial phase (Part 1 of our book series), we'll be using locally stored images. However, in the subsequent part of our book series (Part 2), we'll enhance our catalog by integrating a database to store and manage the images and their attributes. Don't worry about it now.

Before creating a component for Image mapping, first let's create a new folder styles and in that folder create a new style file, ImageMapper.module.css .
Refer to Code 3.1 and copy these styles into , ImageMapper.module.css. We will use these classes in our Image mapper component

Code 3-1: ImageMapper.module.css
```
.imageContainer {
  display: flex;
```

```css
    flex-direction: column;
    justify-content: flex-end;
}
.attribution {
    font-size: 8px;
    color: #666;
    padding-left:5px;
}
```

Now, let's create a dedicated component called ImageMapper.tsx under components folder to handle the mapping of images. This component will serve as a central hub for importing and managing all the images. Refer to the provided code in Code 3.2 and copy it to the new component file. Let's go deep below to that.

Code 3.2: ImageMapper.tsx

```tsx
import handbagBlack from '../images/handbag-black.jpg';
import handbagBrown from '../images/handbag-brown.jpg';
import handbagOrange from '../images/handbag-orange.jpg';
import shoesBlue from '../images/shoes-blue.jpg';
import shoesPink from '../images/shoes-pink.jpg';
import shoesPurple from '../images/shoes-purple.jpg';

import watchBrown from '../images/watch-brown.jpg';
import watchGreen from '../images/watch-green.jpg';
import watchYellow from '../images/watch-yellow.jpg';
import ring from '../images/ring.jpg';

//import styles
import styles from '../styles/ImageMapper.module.css';
// Object mapping names to image URLs
const imageMap: { [key: string]: { url: string;
attribution: string } } = {
```

```typescript
    handbagBlack: { url: handbagBlack, attribution: "Photo
by Laura Chouette on Unsplash" },
    handbagBrown: { url: handbagBrown, attribution: "Photo
by Creative Headline on Unsplash" },
    handbagOrange: { url: handbagOrange, attribution:
"Photo by Arno Senoner on Unsplash" },
    shoesBlue: { url: shoesBlue, attribution: "Photo by
Marcus Lewis on Unsplash" },
    shoesPink: { url: shoesPink, attribution: "Photo by
Marcus Lewis on Unsplash" },
    shoesPurple: { url: shoesPurple, attribution: "Photo
by Marcus Lewis on Unsplash" },
    watchBrown: { url: watchBrown, attribution: "Photo by
WoodWatch on Unsplash" },

    watchGreen: { url: watchGreen, attribution: "Photo by
Bruno van der Kraan on Unsplash" },
    watchYellow: { url: watchYellow, attribution: "Photo
by Marek Prygiel on Unsplash" },
    ring: { url: ring, attribution: "Photo by Sabrianna on
Unsplash" },

};

interface Image {
    name: string;
    width?: string;
    height?: string;
    imageOnly?:boolean;
}

function ImageMapper(props: Image) {
    const {name, width, height, imageOnly} = props;
    // Check if the provided name exists in the imageMap
```

```
    if (imageMap[name]) {
        const { url, attribution } = imageMap[name];
        return <div className={styles.imageContainer}>
            <img src={url} alt={name} width={width}
height={height} />
            {!imageOnly && <span
className={styles.attribution}>@{attribution}</span>}
        </div>;

    } else {
        return <div>No image found for {name}</div>;
    }
}
export default ImageMapper;
```

So here we collated all the images and their respective attribution texts. This component dynamically renders images based on the provided name prop, along with their corresponding attribution text. It's designed to be reusable and flexible for displaying different images throughout the application. If you call this component with image name, width, and height, it will return the image with the attribution text. The attribution is text is conditionally displayed, so that we can avoid having that when we display small images inside Trolley at a later stage.

Import statements import images from the folder. Also we are importing CSS from ImageMapper.module.css. The imageMap object maps image names to their corresponding URLs and attribution text. A Props interface is defined to specify the props expected by the component. We will explain props shortly.

Finally, in the return statement the component renders image and the text.

If you call `<ImageMapper name="handbagBlack" width="350" height="250" />`, it will return the image of the black handbag along with the respective attribution. Similar way, you can pass a different name and get a different image and attribution. Here, the name is a prop. Props allow you to customize what a component displays by passing in specific data or instructions. The `width, height` and `imageOnly`, also props here which are optional. If `imageOnly` is passed with `true` value, the image will be displayed without attribution text, which we will need during Trolley development.

Let's compare this to a real-life scenario to understand props. A Coffee shop (Component) can offer different types of Coffee, such as Latte, Espresso, Cappuccino, Flat white etc. Each customer (Another component of your app) has their own preference. So, they express this preference through a specific order/request. Props are like these specific orders. Props is a way for a component to communicate with another by passing specific instructions.

This is the basic concept of props, and we will learn more about it when we are building the rest of the application. Props play a crucial role in React development by enabling components to be dynamic, reusable, and flexible, facilitating communication between components, and contributing to the building of scalable and maintainable applications.
This completes stage 1 of our Catalog development. We will see the images in the browser once we complete stage 2 & 3.

Building the Item Component

Let's now proceed to stage 3, where we'll craft the item component. This component will showcase essential details of a single product, including its image, name, price, and an option to add it to the cart. These details will be received as props to the item component, allowing it to dynamically display different products based on the data received.

Like we did stage 1, let's create a CSS module for Item component, under the styles folder, and name it as `Item.module.css`. Refer to Code 3.3 and copy the styles.

Code 3.3: Item.module.css

```css
.card {
    display: flex;
    flex-direction: column;
    height: 100%;
    width: 350px;
border:1px solid #d3d3d3;
}
.itemDesc
{
    height:80px;
}
.price {
    padding: 5px 0px 10px 5px;
    font-weight: 600 !important;
}
```

Now, let's proceed to update the Item component code. Initially, we will design the item component. Later, once the Catalog component is developed, we'll integrate it with the item component to render actual product data. Then we can see it in browser. Look at Code 3.4 and replace the current base code in the Item component. We'll discuss its structure and functionality in detail below.

Code 3.4: Item.tsx

```
import { Card, CardContent, Typography, Button } from
'@mui/material';
import AddShoppingCartIcon from '@mui/icons-
material/AddShoppingCart';
import styles from '../styles/Item.module.css';
import ImageMapper from './ImageMapper';

//product specifications
interface Product {
  id: number;
  title: string;
  desc: string;
  imageName: string;
  price: string;
}
function Item(props: Product) {
  const { id, title, desc, imageName, price } = props;
  return (
    <Card className={styles.card} key={id}>
      <ImageMapper name={imageName} width="350"
height="250" />

  <CardContent>
        <Typography variant="h6" component="div">
```

```
            {title}
          </Typography>
          <Typography variant="body2" color="textSecondary"
component="p" className={styles.itemDesc} style={{ height:
'80px' }}>
             {desc}
          </Typography>
          <Typography variant="h6" component="div"
className={styles.price}>
             {price}
          </Typography>
          <Button variant="contained"
endIcon={<AddShoppingCartIcon />}>
             Add to Trolley
          </Button>
        </CardContent>
      </Card>
   );
}
export default Item;
```

Let's go through the component code.

Firstly, We're importing necessary components and icons from the Material-UI library, as well as the CSS module for styling, and the `ImageMapper` component that we've created earlier.

Next, we defined a Product Interface, which defines the structure of our product data. Each product will have an ID, title, description, image name, and price.

Then we defined our function component to take props as input. These props represent the details of a single product. Inside the function, we de-structured the props to extract individual details like the product's ID, title, description, image name, and price.

To render, We're using a Card component from Material-UI to display the product details in a card format. Each card represents a single product. We use the ImageMapper component to display the product image. This component takes the image name as a prop and renders the corresponding image as we described in stage 1.

The CardContent contains the actual content of the card, including the product title, description, and price. We used Typography Component to display text elements with different styles and formats. Then we have a Material-UI Button component with an icon (AddShoppingCartIcon) at the end. It allows users to add the product to their shopping trolley, which we will set up during the Trolley development.

This Item component is responsible for rendering a single product card with its details, including an image, title, description, price, and an option to add it to the trolley.

The Item component is designed to represent a generic product card that can display various product details. It follows the principles of component-based architecture in React, allowing it to be reused multiple times throughout the application. By passing different props to the Item component each time it's used, you can customize its content to display details of various products. For example, you can use the same Item component to display details of a handbag, a pair of shoes, or any other product by providing different props for each instance. We will see this in action next, that is Stage 3.

Constructing the Catalog component

Now, let's move forward to the final stage of Catalog development, where we'll focus on developing the Catalog component. This component will serve as the storefront, displaying all the product details, including images, names, prices, and options to add items to the cart. We'll achieve this by passing the necessary information as props to the Item component, which will then dynamically render each product based on the received data.

Like our previous steps, we'll create a CSS module specifically for the Catalog component to manage its styles. This module will be named `Catalog.module.css` and will be placed under the `styles` folder. Refer to Code 3.5 and copy the styles.

Code 3.5: Catalog.module.css

```
.catalogContainer

{
   padding-top:20px;
}
```

Now, let's proceed to update the Catalog component code. Look at Code 3.6 and replace the current base code in the Catalog component. We'll discuss its structure and functionality in detail below.

Code 3.6: Catalog.tsx

```
//Import MUI component/s
import { Grid } from '@mui/material';

//Import Item component
import Item from './Item';
```

```javascript
// Import CSS modules
import styles from "../styles/Catalog.module.css";

// Set of products
const products = [

  { id: 1, title: "Ferragamo BOXYZ bag", desc: "The
Ferragamo BOXYZ bag in vibrant orange is a timeless
accessory suitable for any occasion with its sleek leather
construction.", imageName: "handbagOrange", price:
"$45.78" },

  { id: 2, title: "Black Michael Kors Tote Bag", desc:
"Chic and versatile, this Michael Kors tote in classic
black is perfect for both office and evening wear.",
imageName: "handbagBlack", price: "$43.50" },
  { id: 3, title: "Diamond Ring", desc: "This exquisite
piece features a silver band that elegantly holds a multi-
stone diamond setting", imageName: "ring", price:
"$923.00" },
  { id: 4, title: "Classic Brown Handbag", desc: "Elegant
in simplicity, this brown handbag pairs well with any
outfit, making it a must-have staple.", imageName:
"handbagBrown", price: "$49.99" },
  { id: 5, title: "Ocean Blue Heels", desc: "Make a
statement with these striking blue heels, perfect for
adding a pop of color to your ensemble.", imageName:
"shoesBlue", price: "$85.00" },
  { id: 6, title: "Pink Ballet Flats", desc: "These
charming pink ballet flats offer comfort without
sacrificing style, ideal for daily wear.", imageName:
"shoesPink", price: "$59.99" },
```

```
  { id: 7, title: "Purple Suede Loafers", desc: "These
luxurious purple suede loafers are the epitome of casual
elegance.", imageName: "shoesPurple", price: "$75.00" },

  { id: 8, title: "Vintage Brown Watch", desc: "A timeless
accessory, this vintage-style watch features a rich brown
leather strap.", imageName: "watchBrown", price: "$110.00"
},
  { id: 9, title: "Emerald Green Timepiece", desc: "This
watch boasts a stunning emerald green face, set in a sleek
silver casing for modern sophistication.", imageName:
"watchGreen", price: "$250.00" },
  { id: 10, title: "Sunny Yellow Watch", desc: "Brighten
your day with this cheerful yellow watch, a perfect blend
of fun and functionality.", imageName: "watchYellow",
price: "$99.00" }
];


function Catalog() {
  return (
    <Grid container className={styles.catalogContainer}
spacing={2} rowGap={2}>
      {products.map((product) => (
        <Grid item key={product.id} xs={6} sm={3} md={4}>
          <Item
            id={product.id}
            title={product.title}

            desc={product.desc}
            imageName={product.imageName}
            price={product.price}
```

```
    />
      </Grid>
    ))}
  </Grid>
  );
}
```

```
export default Catalog;
```

Let's break down the code. The component sets up a catalog display for various products. It imports necessary elements and defines a list of products, each with details like title, description, image, and price. Looking at the return section, the component organizes these products into a grid layout, maintaining a consistent and organized look.

Within the *Catalog*, a Material-UI *Grid* container is used to hold the product items. It loops through each product, creating a grid item for it. Each grid item renders the Item component, passing along the product's details as props. This ensures that the same Item component is reused for displaying each product, promoting code reusability, and maintaining a consistent layout and functionality across all items in the catalog.

This way, the Catalog component showcases products in a catalog format. It arranges items into a responsive grid layout, making them easy to view and navigate. You can define different products with unique titles, descriptions, images, and prices, customizing their catalog to your liking.

The component effortlessly adjusts to any changes in the products array, accommodating varying numbers of products and their attributes.

Save the files before proceeding. Navigate to your web browser and select 'Catalog' from the top menu to preview the catalog's appearance, as shown in Image 3.1.

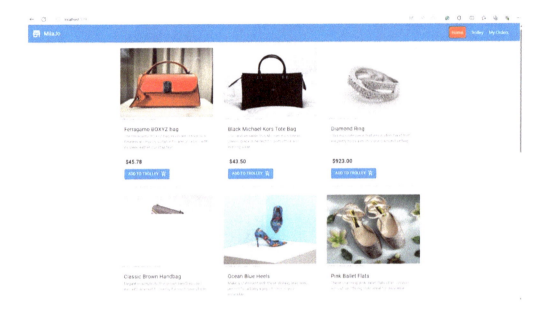

Image 3.1: Catalog component

Within the catalog, you'll find all 10 products neatly arranged, with 3 products displayed in each row. Each product is accompanied by its title, description, image, and price, along with an 'Add to Trolley' button. The Catalog component efficiently renders these products by passing different props to the Item component for each product.

Sip

In this chapter, our primary focus was on understanding and implementing component communication within React. Through the design and development of the Catalog and Item components, we delved into several key features of React.

Firstly, we explored functional components, a simpler and more concise way of defining components in React. Both the Catalog and Item components were designed as functional components, emphasizing the efficiency and clarity they offer in component development.
Next, we discussed the concept of props, which serve to pass data from parent to child components in React. In the Item component specifically, props were utilized to receive crucial product information such as ID, title, description, image name, and price.

Furthermore, we highlighted the stateless nature of functional components, emphasizing their reliance on external data passed via props from parent components. This approach promotes a clean and modular component architecture, enhancing code reusability and maintainability.

Additionally, we underscored the importance of reusable components, particularly showcasing how the Item component can be dynamically utilized within the Catalog component to display various products. This promotes code modularity and scalability.

In terms of TypeScript integration, we leveraged interfaces to define the structure and type of props passed to each component. This ensures robust type checking, enhancing code reliability and development efficiency.

In the upcoming chapter, our attention shifts to the design of the Trolley component, where we'll utilize the 'Add to Trolley' button. Our focus will be on establishing communication between the Catalog and Trolley components, allowing users to effortlessly add items to their shopping trolley directly from the catalog interface. Alongside, we will uncover the power of React Context!

CHAPTER 4

The Aroma of Context

Cup

Step into the aroma of React Context, where we'll be brewing up a fresh batch of knowledge on React. In this chapter, we'll delve into the rich flavors of React context, exploring its functionality and application within our project. We'll start with the creation of a Trolley Provider component, which serves as the cornerstone for managing trolley-related data throughout our application. Within the Item component, we develop the crucial "Add to Trolley" function, seamlessly integrating it with React context to ensure efficient management of trolley items.

Next, we shift our focus to the Trolley component, where users can conveniently view all items added to their trolley, with the flexibility to remove items or proceed with placing an order. Leveraging the power of React context, we establish smooth communication between components, allowing for a smooth user experience. We will also discuss about Effect hook.

Finally, we enhance the Catalog component by incorporating a dynamic Trolley icon, providing users with real-time visibility of the total count of items in their trolley. Through these steps, we unlock the full potential of React context, improving our application with enhanced functionality and user interaction.

React Context

When a user clicks the 'Add to Trolley' button beneath an item, we want to ensure that the item is added to a central place where all selected items are stored, like a shopping trolley. If a user adds the same item multiple times, we should update the quantity in the trolley accordingly.

React Context provides us with a convenient and modern way to manage global state in our React applications. It allows us to create a central data store that can be accessed from any component in our app, making it perfect for our trolley system.

Let's understand What React context is, looking at a real-life example:

Imagine you're on a family vacation to a Gold Coast theme park with numerous rides and attractions. Each ride represents a component in our React application. Now, let's say there's a fun competition among family members to see who can experience the most thrilling rides, and you need to keep track of the availability or queue status across all the rides.

In a traditional React setup, if you wanted to switch from one ride to another, you'd have to relay the ride status information down from the top-level component through every intermediate ride. For instance, imagine you're moving from the 'Vortex' to the 'Jet Rescue Coaster' at Sea World. Between these rides, there are numerous other attractions like the 'Penguin Encounter' and 'Dolphin Presentation'.

This process, much like prop drilling, would necessitate passing the destination ride status as a prop through each intermediate attraction component, even if they don't directly utilize this information. Consequently, managing navigation and passing unnecessary props through multiple components can lead to confusion and inefficiency in handling the state of the rides.

Here's where Context, the master manager of the theme park, gets into the game! The Context acts like a central ride status board, like a theme park map with real-time updates on queue lengths and ride availability. Instead of each ride having to manage its status independently, they can all reference the context to see the current availability or queue status. In our theme park scenario, the context would contain information about the availability or queue status for each ride. Each ride can then update its live status to the context. This allows all family members to conveniently check the context to see the status and join in on the fun.

Brewing Bonds: Implementing React Context

To implement the Trolley functionality in our React app using Context, we'll follow a four-stage process.

Stage 1 - Setting up Context Provider: In this stage, we'll establish the foundation by creating a context provider. This provider will encapsulate the state of the trolley items and expose methods to interact with this state. By wrapping the common parent component of Catalog & Trolley, the App component, with this provider, we enable these components to access and manipulate the trolley state without the need for manual prop passing throughout the component tree.

Stage 2 – Make Item Trolley Ready: In this stage, we'll focus on updating the Item component. Here, we'll modify the Item component to consume the trolley context. Through context, the Item component will gain access to the trolley items and methods required to add or update items in the trolley. With these changes, users will be able to add items to their trolley while browsing the catalog.

Stage 3 – Developing Trolley component: In this stage, we'll create the Trolley component. This component will serve as the interface for users to view the items in their trolley. Leveraging the trolley context, the Trolley component will retrieve the trolley items and display them accordingly. Additionally, it will provide options for users to delete items from their trolley and facilitate the ordering process.

Stage 4 – Adding Trolley Symbol with Item Count: In this final stage, we'll enhance the UI of the Catalog component by introducing a Trolley icon at the bottom. This Trolley icon will feature a badge indicating the total count of items currently in the cart.

Stage 1 - Setting up Context Provider

we'll create a new file called `TrolleyProvider.tsx`. In this file, we'll set up a context to store our trolley items. Using React Context ensures that our trolley data remains synchronized and accessible throughout the app.

To start with, create the new file `TrolleyProvider.tsx`, under `components` folder. Look at Code 4.1 and copy to the item component. We will go through it in detail below:

Code 4.1: TrolleyProvider.tsx

```tsx
import { createContext, Dispatch, SetStateAction,
useState, ReactNode  } from 'react';

interface TrolleyItem {
    id: number;
    title: string;
    imageName: string;
    price: string;
    quantity:number
  }

export const TrolleyContext =
createContext<TrolleyItem[]>([]);
export const TrolleyDispatchContext =
createContext<Dispatch<SetStateAction<TrolleyItem[]>> |
undefined>(undefined);

function TrolleyProvider(props: { children: ReactNode }) {
  const { children } = props;
  const [trolleyItems, setTrolleyItems] =
useState<TrolleyItem[]>([]);

  return (
    <TrolleyContext.Provider value={trolleyItems}>
      <TrolleyDispatchContext.Provider
value={setTrolleyItems}>
        {children}
      </TrolleyDispatchContext.Provider>
    </TrolleyContext.Provider>
  );
}
```

```
export default TrolleyProvider;
```

Let's go through the code.

First, the code imports necessary functions and types from the React library. It defines an interface TrolleyItem which specifies the structure of items that can be added to the shopping trolley. Each item has an `id`, `title`, `imageName`, `price`, and `quantity`.

Next, it creates two contexts using React's `createContext` function. The `TrolleyContext` is created to hold an array of `TrolleyItem` objects, representing the items currently in the trolley. The `TrolleyDispatchContext` context is created to hold a function that can be used to update the trolley items. These contexts are exported so they can be accessed by other components.

If you think about our theme park example, `TrolleyContext` holds the ride status board, which is represented by `trolleyItems`. The `TrolleyDispatchContext` holds the software system for the rides to update ride status board.

The `TrolleyDispatchContext` serves as the control center for managing updates to the ride status board. Think of it as the control panel where operators/software can adjust the status of each ride based on real-time information. The `TrolleyDispatchContext` allows components to dynamically update the trolley items in response to user actions, such as adding or updating items from the shopping trolley.

Below is the explanation of how we defined this `TrolleyDispatchContext`.

`SetStateAction` is a utility type provided by React to define the valid types that can be passed to the updater function returned by the `useState` hook. It ensures type safety when updating state in React components. | `undefined` indicates that the context may initially have no value, represented by undefined. And (undefined) is the initial value of the context, which is set to undefined.

We have the `TrolleyProvider` component defined next. This component wraps its children with the contexts we created earlier. It uses `useState` hook to manage the state of the trolley items. Initially, the trolley items state is an empty array. The component provides the trolley items state and the function to update it to the respective contexts.

Finally, the `TrolleyProvider` component is exported as the default export of the module. This allows other components in the application to import and use it. By wrapping parts of the application in the `TrolleyProvider`, those components gain access to the trolley state and can interact with it without having to pass props down through the component tree manually.

Next, we need to wrap our App component with the `TrolleyProvider`, so that both the `Catalog` & the `Trolley` component has access to it. So, modify App component, by adding the below snippets.

1) Add the below import.

   ```
   import TrolleyProvider from "./TrolleyProvider;
   ```

2) Wrap the JSX with 'TrolleyProvider'. So the 'return' function outer layer will be like below.

   ```
   <TrolleyProvider>
     <Router>
   ```

```
      <div>
        .....

      </div>
      <Router>
    <TrolleyProvider>
```

This completes our Stage 1 of setting up Trolley functionality/React context.

Stage 2 – Make Item Trolley Ready

To enable the 'Add to Trolley' functionality in the Item component, we need to implement a mechanism, where clicking on the button triggers an action to add or update items in the Trolley context. Code 4.2 shows the modified Item component that reflects this change. Below to the code section, let us discuss the modifications made.

```
Code 4.2: Item.tsx
import { useContext, useState } from 'react';
import { Card, CardContent, Typography, Button, Snackbar,
Alert } from '@mui/material';
import AddShoppingCartIcon from '@mui/icons-
material/AddShoppingCart';
import styles from '../styles/Item.module.css';
import ImageMapper from './ImageMapper';

//Import Contexts
import { TrolleyContext, TrolleyDispatchContext } from
"./TrolleyProvider";

interface Product {
  id: number;

  title: string;
```

```typescript
  desc: string;
  imageName: string;
  price: string;
}

function Item(props: Product) {
  const { id, title, desc, imageName, price } = props;
  const trolleyItems = useContext(TrolleyContext);
  const setTrolleyItems =
useContext(TrolleyDispatchContext);
  const [snackbarOpen, setSnackbarOpen] = useState(false);
  const [snackbarMessage, setSnackbarMessage] =
useState<string>("");

  // Function to add item to trolley
  const addToTrolley = (product: Product) => {
    if (setTrolleyItems) {
      setTrolleyItems(prevItems => {
        const existingItemIndex = prevItems.findIndex(item
=> item.id === product.id);
        if (existingItemIndex !== -1) {
          // Item already exists, update the count
          const updatedItems = [...prevItems];
          updatedItems[existingItemIndex].quantity += 1;

      setSnackbarMessage(`${title} is updated in
trolley`);
          setSnackbarOpen(true);
          return updatedItems;
        } else {
          // Item doesn't exist, add it to the trolley
          const newItem = { ...product, quantity: 1 };
          setSnackbarMessage(`${title} is added to
trolley`);
```

```
            setSnackbarOpen(true);
            return [...prevItems, newItem];
        }
      });
    }
  };

  const handleCloseSnackbar = () => {
    setSnackbarOpen(false); // Close snackbar
  };

  return (
    <TrolleyContext.Provider value={trolleyItems}>
      <Card className={styles.card} key={id}>
        <ImageMapper name={imageName} width="350"
height="250" />
        <CardContent>
          <Typography variant="h6" component="div">
            {title}

          </Typography>
          <Typography variant="body2"
color="textSecondary" component="p"
className={styles.itemDesc} style={{ height: '80px' }}>
            {desc}
          </Typography>
          <Typography variant="h6" component="div"
className={styles.price}>
            {price}
          </Typography>
          <Button variant="contained" onClick={() =>
addToTrolley(props)} endIcon={<AddShoppingCartIcon />}>
            Add to Trolley
          </Button>
```

```
        </CardContent>
      </Card>
      <Snackbar open={snackbarOpen}
autoHideDuration={3000} onClose={handleCloseSnackbar}>
        <Alert variant="filled"
onClose={handleCloseSnackbar} severity="success">
          {snackbarMessage}
        </Alert>
      </Snackbar>
    </TrolleyContext.Provider>
  );
}
export default Item;
```

Let's look at each change we made.

The Item component now integrates the `TrolleyContext` and `TrolleyDispatchContext` imported from the `TrolleyProvider` component. By utilizing React's `useContext` hook, it gains access to the `TrolleyContext`, which holds information about the items in the trolley, as well as the TrolleyDispatchContext, enabling it to update the trolley items as needed.

1) An update has been made to the functionality of the `Add to Trolley` button within the Item component. Now, when clicked, it triggers the `addToTrolley` function, passing the product props along as arguments. This action initiates the process of adding the product to the trolley.

2) The `addToTrolley` function is defined within the component, responsible for adding or updating items in the trolley. It checks if the `setTrolleyItems` function is available and then updates the trolley

state accordingly. If the item being added already exists in the trolley, it updates the quantity; otherwise, it adds a new item to the trolley.

3) A new feature has been introduced in the form of a Snackbar component within the Item component. This Snackbar serves to display a brief message whenever an item is successfully added or updated in the trolley. This provides immediate feedback to the user regarding their interaction with the trolley.

Previously, the Item component displayed product information. Now it has the added functionality of interacting with the trolley through React context.

Stage 3 – Developing Trolley component

Let's design the Trolley component. It will present a list of items that have been added, showing their quantity, price, and total price. Each item will have a delete option for removal from the trolley. At this stage, we won't offer the ability to update individual item quantities.

Users will be able to enter an email address to receive payment instructions and order confirmation. While we won't implement the email functionality immediately, we'll display a message upon clicking the "Place Order" button.

After placing the order, we'll clear the trolley, displaying a message that the order has been successfully placed. Later, the user can see the order details and status from My Orders page, which we will be developing in the next chapter.

First, let's create a CSS module specifically for the Trolley component to manage its styles. Create a file Trolley.module.css, under the styles folder. Refer to Code 4.3 and copy the styles.

Code 4.3: Trolley.module.css

```css
.trolleyContainer {
  padding: 20px;
  border: 1px solid #ccc;
  border-radius: 5px;
  background-color: #f9f9f9;
  margin-top:30px;
}
.itemsContainer {
  margin-bottom: 20px;
}
.item {
  display: flex;
  align-items: center;
}
.itemImage {
  width: 50px;
  height: 50px;
  object-fit: cover;
  margin-right: 10px;
}
.itemDetails {
  flex-grow: 1;
  padding-left:20px;
}
.totalPrice {
  font-size: 20px;
  margin-bottom: 10px;
  color:green;
  margin-bottom: 20px;
```

```css
}
.emailInput {
  margin-bottom: 20px   !important;
  background-color: white;
}
.checkoutButton {
    width: 20%;
    background-color: rgb(223, 76, 213) !important;
    margin-right:30px !important;
    color:white !important
}
.deleteIcon
{
  color:#FF5733;
  padding-top:20px;
  cursor: pointer;
}
```

Now, let's create the Trolley functionality. Start by replacing the code for the Trolley component from Code 4.4. We'll review and discuss the code details in the following steps.

Code 4.4: Trolley.tsx
```tsx
import { useContext, useEffect, useState } from 'react'
import { TrolleyContext, TrolleyDispatchContext } from
"./TrolleyProvider";
import { Grid, TextField, Button, Snackbar, Alert } from
'@mui/material';
import DeleteForever from '@mui/icons-
material/DeleteForever';
import ImageMapper from './ImageMapper';
import styles from '../styles/Trolley.module.css';

const Trolley = () => {
```

```javascript
  const trolleyItems = useContext(TrolleyContext);
  const setTrolleyItems =
useContext(TrolleyDispatchContext);
  const [email, setEmail] = useState('');
  const [price, setPrice] = useState('');
  const [openSuccessSnackbar, setOpenSuccessSnackbar] =
useState(false);

    useEffect(() => {
    const calculateTotalPrice = () => {
      let totalPrice = 0;
      trolleyItems.forEach(item => {
        const price = parseFloat(item.price.replace('$',
'')));
        totalPrice += price * item.quantity;
      });
      const finalPrice = `$${totalPrice.toFixed(2)}`;
      setPrice(finalPrice);
    }
    calculateTotalPrice();
  }, [trolleyItems]);

  const handlePlaceOrder = () => {
    setOpenSuccessSnackbar(true);
  };

  const handleCloseSuccessSnackbar = () => {
    setOpenSuccessSnackbar(false);
    if (setTrolleyItems) {

    setTrolleyItems([]);
    }
  };
  const handleDeleteItem = (itemId: number) => {
```

```
  if (setTrolleyItems) {
      setTrolleyItems(prevItems => prevItems.filter(item
=> item.id !== itemId));
    }
 };
 const validateEmail = (email: string) => {
    // Regular expression for email validation
    const emailRegex = /^[^\s@]+@[^\s@]+\.[^\s@]+$/;
    return emailRegex.test(email);
 };
const validateAddress = (address: string) => {
    if (!address.trim()) {
      return false;
    }
    return true;
 };
 return (
    <div className={styles.trolleyContainer}>
      {trolleyItems.length === 0 ? (
        <div>
          No items in the Trolley. To add items to your
trolley, visit the catalog.
        </div>
      ) : (<>
        <Grid container spacing={2}
className={styles.itemsContainer}>
          {trolleyItems.map((item) => (

            <Grid item key={item.id} xs={12} sm={12}
className={styles.item}>
              <ImageMapper name={item.imageName}
width="40" height="40" imageOnly={true} />
              <div className={styles.itemDetails}>
                <div>{item.title}</div>
```

```
          <div>
            Quantity: {item.quantity}
            {', '}
            Price:
${(parseFloat(item.price.replace('$', '')) *
item.quantity).toFixed(2)}
          </div>
        </div>
        <DeleteForever onClick={() =>
handleDeleteItem(item.id)} className={styles.deleteIcon}
/>
      </Grid>
    ))}
  </Grid>
 <div className={styles.totalPrice}>{price && `Total
Amount: ${price}`}</div>
 <TextField
        label="Enter Email"
        variant="outlined"
        required
        fullWidth
        className={styles.emailInput}
        type="email"
        value={email}

  onChange={(e) => setEmail(e.target.value)}
        error={!validateEmail(email)}
      />

   <TextField
        label="Enter Shipping Address"
        variant="outlined"
        required
        fullWidth
```

```jsx
          className={styles.emailInput}
          type="text"
          value={address}
          onChange={(e) => setAddress(e.target.value)}
          error={!validateAddress(address)}
        />
        <Button
          variant="contained"
          color="primary"
          onClick={handlePlaceOrder}
          className={styles.checkoutButton}
          disabled={!validateAddress(address) &&
!validateEmail(email)}
        >
          Place Order
        </Button>
      </>
      )}
      <Snackbar open={openSuccessSnackbar}
autoHideDuration={6000}
onClose={handleCloseSuccessSnackbar}>

        <Alert onClose={handleCloseSuccessSnackbar}
severity="success" variant="filled" >
          Order successfully placed. You can view the
order details from My Orders page.
        </Alert>
      </Snackbar>
    </div>
  );
};

export default Trolley;
```

Let's break down the Trolley component code:

Imports and Context: We start by importing the necessary hooks and components. We also import the `TrolleyContext` and `TrolleyDispatchContext` from the `TrolleyProvider`, which provide access to the trolley items and a function to update them, respectively. As we mentioned before, these contexts help us manage the global state of the trolley across different components.

State Management: We use the `useState` hook to manage local state variables within the component. Here, we initialize state variables for the user's email address and whether to show the success snackbar upon placing an order.

Rendering Trolley Items: Inside the component, we render the list of trolley items using the Grid component from Material-UI. For each item, we display its details such as image, title, quantity, and calculated price. Additionally, we include a delete icon for each item, which users can click to remove the item from the trolley.

Handling User Actions: We defined functions to handle user actions such as placing an order, closing the success snack bar, deleting an item from the trolley, calculating total price, and validating the user's email and address. These functions update the component's state and interact with the trolley state through the provided dispatch function. We are calculating total price during any change in `trolleyItems`. This is achieved using the `useEffect` hook.

Order Placement: When the user clicks the `Place Order` button, we trigger the `handlePlaceOrder` function to display the success snack bar and clear the trolley items. The snack bar provides feedback to the user that the order is successfully placed, and they can view the placed order details from My Orders page. Then it will empty the Trolley.

In the current phase, the My Orders page doesn't display any content, but don't worry, we'll address that in the upcoming chapter. For now, users can add items to their trolley, input their email, place the order, and view a success message. Although we've included email and address inputs, note that it's just to add a touch of realism to the order process, no actual emails will be sent.

After wrapping up the first three stages of implementing the Trolley functionality, it's time to see it in action within the browser. Once you're done testing, we'll move on to the final stage, which includes enhancing the catalog user interface. Remember to save your changes. If npm start isn't running yet, fire it up in the terminal.

You can now browse the home page and add items to your Trolley from the catalog. Refer to image 4.1, where I am adding an item to the Trolley, and it displays the snack bar message.

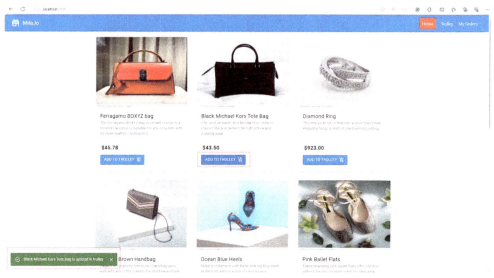

Image 4.1: Add an item to Trolley

By clicking on the Trolley in the top navigation, you can access a summary of the items in their Trolley, including their quantities and total price. You have the option to delete items from the Trolley or proceed to place an order.

Referencing Image 4.2, it serves as an example of how the Trolley might appear, displaying the added items and their details.

Image 4.2: Trolley

You can input email and address, and then click on the button to place the order. It will display the message for 6 seconds and then clear the trolley.

Through this practical implementation, we have effectively learned the concept of React context, utilizing it to manage state and facilitate communication between components without the need for prop drilling. In the next step, we will consume the context from the Catalog component to display trolley items count in that page.

Before moving on to the next step, as we used useEffect hook first time in this app, let me explain you a bit detail about that.

useEffect hook

The useEffect hook in React allows you to perform side effects in function components! The When you use useEffect, you provide a function as the first argument, which will execute after the component has rendered. The second argument, known as the dependency array, determines when the effect should run. If the dependency array is empty, the effect runs only once after the initial render. If it contains values, the effect will execute whenever any of those values change between renders.

Consider the code snippet below:

```
useEffect(() => {
    console.log('Component loaded for the first time');
}, []);
```

In this example, we pass an empty array as the second argument, indicating that the effect should run only on the initial component load. Here's how it works: during the first render, the effect runs because the array is empty. On subsequent renders, the array remains empty, so the effect doesn't run again. This behavior ensures that the effect runs only once.

In our Trolley component, we use useEffect to recalculate the total price whenever the trolleyItems array changes. By specifying trolleyItems as a dependency, we ensure that the effect runs whenever this array changes, keeping our UI up to date with the latest data.

Stage 4 - Trolley Symbol with Item Count

In this final stage for Trolley step, let's add a UI enhancement to the Catalog component. We'll incorporate a Trolley icon at the bottom, complete with a badge displaying the total count of items in the Trolley dynamically. To implement this, we need to update the Catalog component code.

Refer to Code 4.5 to review the updated *Catalog.tsx* code. Below, I'll outline each change made within this update. Since there are no modifications to the Products array, that part is skipped in the below code sections. So, rather than duplicating the entire code segment, go through only the amended parts and update your code accordingly. In Code 4.5, I marked the changes using the comments starting with //New.

Code 4.5: Catalog.tsx

```
import { Grid } from '@mui/material';
import Item from './Item';
import styles from "../styles/Catalog.module.css";

//New - Imports for Trolley badges
import { Badge } from '@mui/material';
import ShoppingCartCheckoutIcon from '@mui/icons-
material/ShoppingCartCheckout';
import { useNavigate } from 'react-router-dom';
import { useContext } from 'react';
import { TrolleyContext } from "./TrolleyProvider";
// Set of products
const products = [];
//keep the products here as in the code listing in Chapter
3 (Code 3.6)



function Catalog() {

  //New - declarations
  const navigate = useNavigate();
  const trolleyItems = useContext(TrolleyContext);

  return (
```

```jsx
    <>
        <Grid container className={styles.catalogContainer}
spacing={2} rowGap={2}>
            {products.map((product) => (
                <Grid item key={product.id} xs={6} sm={3}
md={4}>
                    <Item
                        id={product.id}
                        title={product.title}
                        desc={product.desc}
                        imageName={product.imageName}
                        price={product.price}
                    />
                </Grid>
            ))}
        </Grid>

        <div className={styles.trolleyIconContainer}>
            <Badge badgeContent={trolleyItems.reduce((total,
item) => total + item.quantity, 0)} color="success"
overlap="circular" onClick={() => navigate('/trolley')} >
                <ShoppingCartCheckoutIcon
className={styles.trolleyIcon} />
            </Badge>
        </div>
    </>
    );
}

export default Catalog;
```

Let's go through each change.

<u>Change 1:</u> We added a few new lines to imports section.

The `Badge` & `ShoppingCartCheckoutIcon` imports allows us to display a badge icon, which can indicate notifications or item counts. The import `useNavigate` from react-router-dom is to navigate to the Trolley component when the badge is clicked.

Additionally, we use `useContext` to access context values provided by the `TrolleyProvider` component, allowing us to retrieve information about the items added to the trolley. Finally, the `TrolleyContext` import from `TrolleyProvider` enables us to access the Trolley context, facilitating the retrieval of trolley items and determining the count to display on the badge.

<u>Change 2:</u> We added the below two declarations inside the `Catalog` function.

```
const navigate = useNavigate();
const trolleyItems = useContext(TrolleyContext);
```

We'll use `navigate` to direct users to the Trolley component when the Trolley icon is clicked. The `trolleyItems` utilizes the `useContext()` hook to access the trolley-related data stored in the `TrolleyProvider` context, just like we did in the Trolley component earlier (Stage 3). This allows us to retrieve information about items currently in the trolley, enabling dynamic updates to the Trolley badge displayed in the Catalog component.

<u>Change 3:</u> We added the Badge functionality by appending a `div` section next to the `Grid` section inside the return statement.

In this code snippet, we have a Badge component wrapping our ShoppingCartCheckoutIcon, representing the trolley icon. The badgeContent prop is now set to the total quantity of items in the trolleyItems array, calculated by summing up the quantity property of each item. This ensures that the badge count dynamically updates to reflect the total quantity of items in the trolley, considering the quantity of each individual item.

Additionally, we've specified the color of the badge to be success and set the overlap prop to circular to ensure the badge neatly encircles the icon. Finally, we've attached an onClick event handler to the badge, triggering the navigate function when the icon is clicked, directing the user to the Trolley component. We will add the CSS module classes we used in this section to Catalog.module.css, shortly.

You might have noticed that, in the updated code, we've enclosed the Grid and div elements within a React Fragment (<></>). A Fragment is a feature provided by React that allows us to group multiple elements without introducing an additional node to the DOM. By using a Fragment, we can structure our JSX code more efficiently without affecting the HTML output. In this case, wrapping the Grid and div elements in a Fragment was necessary to ensure that they are rendered as siblings without introducing any unnecessary parent elements. This helps maintain a cleaner and more organized structure in the rendered output.

So, let's add the below classes to Catalog.module.css. Refer to Code 4.6

Code 4.6: Catalog.module.css

```
.trolleyIconContainer {
    position: fixed;
    bottom: 20px;
    right: 20px;
```

```
  z-index: 1000;
  cursor: pointer;
}
.trolleyIcon {
  color: #ff5733;
  font-size: 50px !important;
}
```

Now, let's look at the browser, where you'll notice the Trolley icon positioned at the bottom right of the catalog screen. As you add items to your trolley, the badge count will increase accordingly, displaying the total number of items added. If you happen to add the same item more than once, the badge count will accurately reflect the total quantity. Refer to Image 4.3.

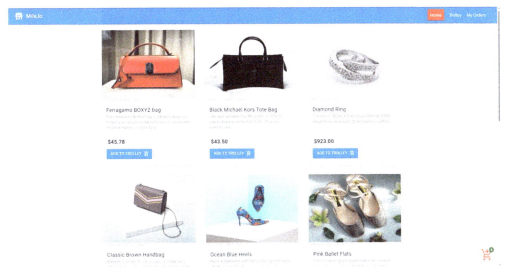

Image 4.3 Trolley Count display in Catalog

When you're ready to proceed to checkout, simply click on the icon, and you'll be redirected to the Trolley details page. Upon redirection, you'll observe that the top navigation updates to display 'Trolley', providing a fluid transition to the trolley interface.

Sip

In this chapter, we explored React context, a crucial part of building React applications. With context, you can share data between components without having to explicitly pass it through every level of the component tree. This makes your code cleaner, more efficient, and easier to maintain, especially in large applications where prop drilling can become cumbersome.

After learning about context, you understand how to keep track of data across your app using providers and consumers. In our app, the Item component provided the context, whereas Trolley and Catalog components consumed it.

With the Trolley provider, you can easily manage items in your shopping cart from anywhere in the app. Plus, the Trolley component lets us see and interact with our cart items, making it easy to shop and place orders. And by adding a Trolley icon to the Catalog, we can now quickly see how many items are in our cart.

Overall, this chapter provided you with an understanding of how to establish a centralized state management system using React Context. In the process, it transformed how our app works, making it more organized and user-friendly. You also learned about how useEffect hook works.

In the next chapter, we'll explore the creation of the "My Orders" component, an essential tool for users to monitor their previous and current orders. Along the way, I'll introduce you to MERN stack and delve deeper into various React features, enriching your understanding of app development.

CHAPTER 5

The MERN Blend

Cup

In this chapter, we'll delve into the world of MERN stack development, which encompasses MongoDB, Express.js, React.js, and Node.js. Our primary focus will be on implementing the My Orders functionality within our application. We'll start by setting up a MongoDB database and creating a dedicated collection to store orders. Moving forward, we'll configure the server-side environment using Node.js and Express, establishing smooth interaction between the server and the database. To ensure the functionality is working as expected, we'll leverage the VS Code ThunderClient extension to test our API endpoints.

Once the server setup is complete, we'll shift our attention back to the client-side code. Here, we'll enhance the Trolley component to initiate an order placement process. This will involve making a call to the server, triggering the order route, and subsequently creating an order entry in the database. Additionally, we'll develop the "My Orders" page, where users can view their past orders. For testing purposes, we'll use a predefined test user throughout this chapter, with plans to implement a user-specific order system in the subsequent chapter, focusing on authentication.

By the end of this chapter, you'll gain valuable insights into the MERN stack and how to establish robust connections between the database, server, and client. Through practical implementation, you'll learn essential concepts of full-stack development and enhance your understanding of building dynamic web applications.

Introduction to MERN Stack

The MERN stack is like a toolbox for building websites. Each tool serves a specific purpose:

1) **M**ongoDB: Think of MongoDB as a smart storage space. It is the database where we store our data. It keeps all our website's data organized and easy to find. It's like having a giant filing cabinet where we can store information in a structured way.

2) **Express:** Express is a web framework for Node.js. It simplifies the process of handling HTTP requests, routing, middleware integration, and other server-side operations in Node.js. It is a bit like the framework of a house that holds everything together and makes sure it runs smoothly.

3) **React**: Obviously now you know what React is! React makes our website look great and work smoothly. It's like the magic paintbrush that we use to create all the different parts of our website, from buttons and forms to entire pages. We're in chapter 5 now, piecing together the other tools to bring our website to life.

4) **N**ode.js: Node.js is the engine that powers everything. It takes care of all the behind-the-scenes work, like handling requests from users and talking to the database. It's like the electricity that keeps our website running smoothly.

So, when you use the MERN stack, you're essentially combining these four essential ingredients to brew up a fantastic web application, just like brewing a delicious cup of coffee.

Tackling the Order Challenge

To save and retrieve user-specific orders, we need to follow a series of steps using various technologies.

1) Managing Orders: When the user clicks the "place order" button, the order details need to be stored in a database. This includes specifying an order ID, ordered items, status, quantity, email, shipping address, and the user's name. Initially, as we don't have the user's name, we'll use a constant value, globalUser. This information will be structured as a JSON object and saved to a MongoDB collection named 'orders'. Collections in MongoDB store data, and each one is specific to a particular database. To accomplish this, we'll establish server-side code using Node.js to communicate with MongoDB, transitioning our project to the MERN Stack.

Next, we need to design the My Orders page which displays orders specific to a user, detailing each order. We'll query the orders from MongoDB database using Node.js to fetch order details. Initially, we'll retrieve all orders since we have only one user (say, globalUser).

2) Sign Up: Users can sign up using their name, username, and password. We'll create a SignUp React component and save user details to another MongoDB collection named 'users'. Passport.js is a popular authentication middleware for Node.js applications. It provides a simple and flexible way to authenticate users using different strategies, such as username and password, OAuth authentication with providers like Google, Facebook, and many others. In our scenario, Passport.js will be configured to authenticate users against the 'users' collection in MongoDB, ensuring that only authorized users can sign up and access the application's features.

3) Log In: Authentication will allow users to log in using their username and password. We'll utilize passport.js to authenticate users against the 'users' collection in MongoDB.

4) <u>Linking User to the Order</u>: The MyOrders component will be updated to use the actual username instead of globalUser. When saving an order, we'll store the username along with other details. For fetching user-specific orders, we'll use the logged-in username instead of globalUser. Authentication using passport will ensure security during order save and fetch operations, completing the My Orders functionality.

5) <u>Log Out</u>: We'll implement log-out functionality for users.

In this chapter, our focus is on step 1, which involves laying the foundation for our MERN Stack project by managing orders. We'll store orders in a MongoDB database. By establishing server-side code with Node.js, we'll create a communication bridge between our application and MongoDB. This allows us to store order information in a MongoDB collection named 'orders'. Additionally, we'll design the My Orders page to display orders specific to a user, initially fetching all orders since we only have one user.

Steps 2 to 5, which involve user authentication, signing up, logging in, linking users to orders, and implementing log out functionality, will be covered in Chapter 6. In that chapter, we'll dive into authentication using passport.js and further extend our MERN stack development.

Managing Orders

Saving the orders involves 3 sub-stages.

<u>Stage 1: Database Setup with MongoDB</u>: Initially, we'll create a MongoDB database. Within this database, we'll establish a dedicated collection named "orders" to store our order data.

Stage 2: Server-side Configuration: Next, we'll configure the server-side environment for our React application. This involves setting up Node.js to interact with the "orders" collection we created earlier, enabling seamless communication between the server and the database.

Stage 3: Save Orders: Returning to our React code, we'll enhance the Trolley component to structure an order object. Subsequently, we'll initiate an API request to the server, facilitating the storage of the order within the designated collection in the database.

Stage 4: Retrieve Orders: In this phase, we'll focus on the My Orders component. Here, we'll configure it to retrieve orders associated with the globalUser. The retrieved orders will then be presented in a user-friendly format for seamless browsing.

Stage 1: Database Setup with MongoDB

To set up a MongoDB database, we can use a free tier provided by Atlas. Go to https://www.mongodb.com/cloud/atlas/register and create your Atlas account. Click on 'Try Free' on the top right once you log in.

You will be taken to Deploy your database screen. Select M0, the free Tier. Provide a name Cluster-MilaJo for the cluster. You can use a different name for the cluster. Leave other settings as it is and click on Create Deployment. Refer to Image 5.1.

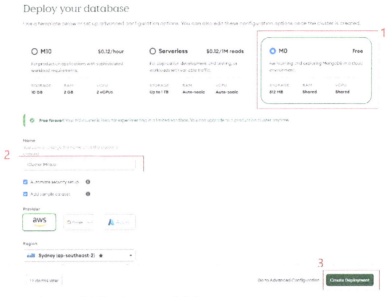

Image 5.1 Deploy your database.

A popup screen will appear. We need to create a database user at this step. You can update the username and password or leave it as it is. Copy username and password to a notepad for now. Then, click on Create Database User button. Then, click on Choose a connection method. Steps highlighted in Image 5.2.

Connect to Cluster-MilaJo

Set up connection security — Choose a connection method — Connect

You need to secure your MongoDB Atlas cluster before you can use it. Set which users and IP addresses can access your cluster now. Read more ☑

1. **Add a connection IP address**

   ✅ Your current IP address (▮▮▮▮▮) has been added to enable local connectivity.

2. **Create a database user**

   This first user will have atlasAdmin ☑ permissions for this project. You'll need your database user's credentials in the next step.

   We autogenerated a username and password. You can use this or create your own.

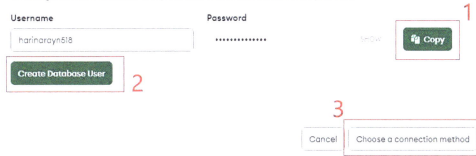

Username	Password
harinarayn518	••••••••••••• SHOW 📋 Copy **1**

Create Database User **2**

3

Cancel | Choose a connection method

Image 5.2 Create database user.

In the next screen `Connect to your application`, choose `Drivers` option. Refer to Image 5.3

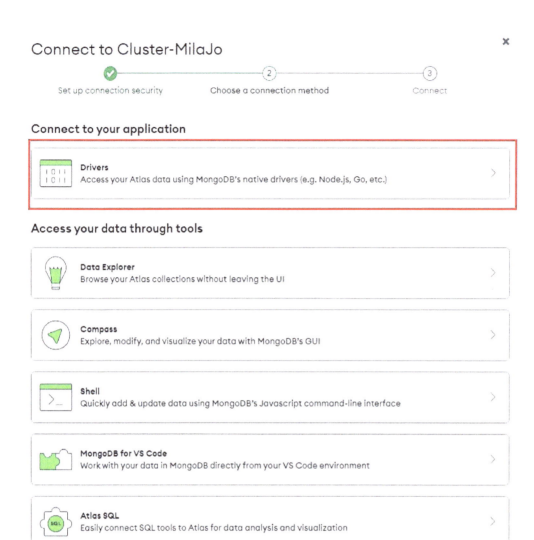

Image 5.3 Select Drivers option

Now, it will show you the connection string in the next screen. Just copy it to your notepad, and then you can close the popup. Refer to Image 5.4

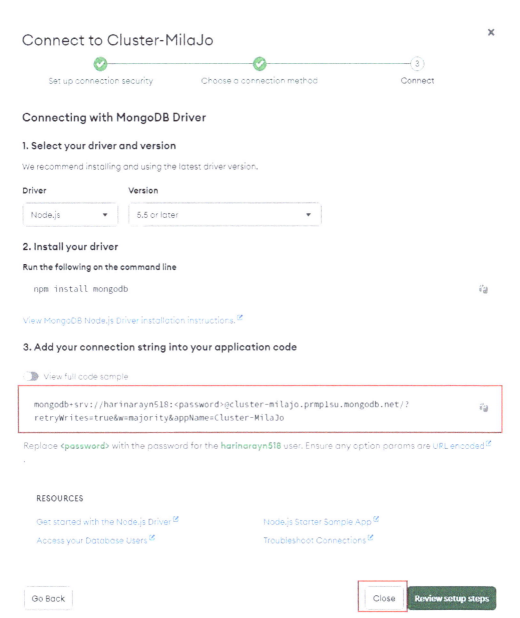

Image 5.4 Copy connection string.

Next, you will be taken to your Data services Dashboard. Click on Browse collections. Refer to image 5.5.

Image 5.5 Dashboard

Next, you'll be directed to the database collections screen where you can create our collection. In this interface, you'll notice sample databases and collections, which you can disregard. Simply click on Create Database, specify the name as db-milajo, set the collection name as orders, and then click on Create. Refer to Image 5.6 for visual guidance.

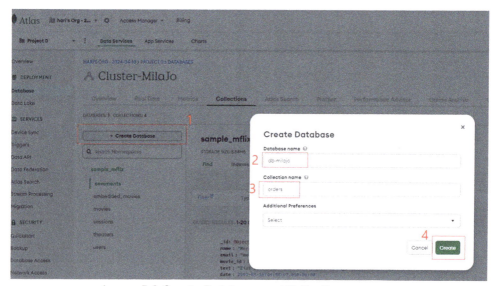

Image 5.6 Create Database and Collection

Now, we have the database and collection ready to host our orders. Let's move on to the next stage!

Stage 2: Server-side Configuration

Now that our database is set up, the next step is to configure the server to enable communication between the app and the database. Currently, our project only consists of client-side code. To begin, navigate to your project directory in Windows Explorer and create two new folders named `client` and `server`. Refer to Image 5.7 for guidance.

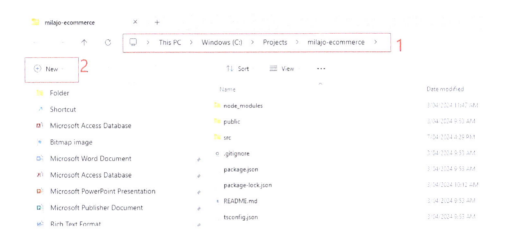

Image 5.7 Create client and server folders.

Now, transfer all your existing code to the `client` folder. Ensure to close the project in Visual Studio Code before making this move. Refer to Image 5.8 for a visual guide.

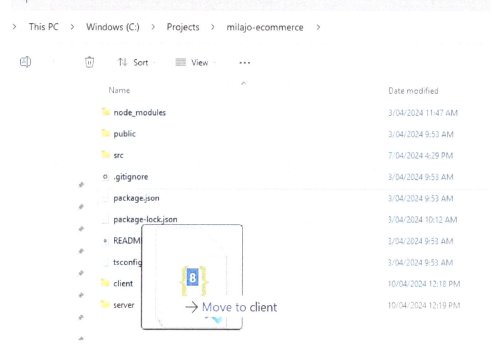

Image 5.8 Create Database and Collection

Open the project folder in Visual Studio Code. Open the terminal and run cd
server to move to server folder. Then run npm init -y. This will create a
package.json file. Replace the contents of package.json with the below.
Refer to Code 5.1.

Code 5.1 package.json (server)

```
{
  "name": "milajo-ecommerce",
  "version": "1.0.0",
  "description": "",
  "main": "index.js",
  "scripts": {
    "start": "node index.js",
    "build-start": "cd.. && cd client && npm run build &&
cd .. && cd server && node index.js"  },
  "keywords": [],
```

```
  "author": "",
  "license": "ISC",
  "dependencies": {
    "bcrypt": "^5.1.1",
    "body-parser": "^1.20.2",
    "connect-mongo": "^5.1.0",
    "cors": "^2.8.5",
    "dotenv": "^16.4.5",
    "express": "^4.19.2",
    "express-session": "^1.18.0",
    "mongodb": "^6.5.0",
    "mongoose": "^8.3.1",
    "passport": "^0.7.0",
    "passport-local": "^1.0.0"  }
```

The package.json lists all the dependencies required by the project. Also, we defined a script to start the server. Also, we added a build-start script. This will automate the process of building the client-side React app, then navigating to the server directory and starting the server. This ensures that the client-side code is compiled and optimized before the server starts serving it to users.

Moving on to the dependencies section, in addition to the MongoDB packages, we included the dependencies such a passport, bcrypt etc for later use in authentication. Now go to the terminal, ensure that you are in server folder and run npm install. This will install all the required packages for the server.

Next, let us create an .env file under the server folder. Copy the below content into the file.

```
CONN_STRING= mongodb+srv://{your-username}:{your-password}@cluster-milajo.prmp1su.mongodb.net/ db-milajo?retryWrites=true&w=majority&appName=Cluster-MilaJo
PORT=8080
```

So, we stored database URL (CONN_STRING) and the server port inside this file. It is important to replace {your-username} and {your-password} with your respective username and password. Also verify the database name (db-milajo) cluster URL and cluster name with that of yours with the copied connection string on Stage 1.1. If there are any changes, ensure that it is also replaced in your code. Also, If your password contains special characters like #, make sure to encode them.

For example, if your password is password#876, it should be written as password%23876.

The .env file typically contains key-value pairs of environment variables in the format KEY=VALUE, where each line represents a separate variable.
The purpose of using environment variables and creating a .env file is to provide a convenient and secure way to manage configuration settings for your application. By using environment variables, you can separate sensitive or environment-specific information from your codebase, such as API keys, database URIs, authentication credentials, and other configuration parameters.

We need to use require('dotenv').config() in the JS file where you are using environment variables. It loads the .env file and makes its contents available as environment variables within your application. This allows you to access these variables using process.env.VARIABLE_NAME.

Next step is creating a module to connect to the database. Create a folder db under server folder. Then, create a file connection.js. Copy the code from Code 5.2 to connection.js. let's break down the code below to that.

Code 5.2 connection.js
```
const mongoose = require("mongoose");
require("dotenv").config();
const connString = process.env.CONN_STRING;
```

```
mongoose.set("strictQuery", true, "useNewUrlParser",
true);

const connectDB = async () => {
  try {
    await mongoose.connect(connString);
  } catch (err) {
    console.error(err.message);
  }
};
module.exports = connectDB;
```

The provided code is a Node.js module responsible for connecting to a
MongoDB database using Mongoose, a MongoDB object modeling tool
designed to work in an asynchronous environment. It first imports the
mongoose module and defines the database credentials, including the
password and database name.

These credentials are used to construct the MongoDB connection URI, which
includes the username, password, database name, cluster name. The
connectDB function is then defined as an asynchronous function that
attempts to establish a connection to the MongoDB database using the
provided URI from the environment file. If the connection is successful, no
action is taken. Otherwise, any encountered errors are logged to the console.
Finally, the connectDB function is exported from the module, allowing it to
be imported and used in other parts of the application to establish a
connection to the MongoDB database.

So now we have the DB connection defined, the next step is to create a model
for the order. Create a new folder models and create a new file Order.js
inside that. Use the code from Code 5.3 for the contents of this file.

```
Code 5.3 Order.js
const mongoose = require("mongoose");

const OrderSchema = new mongoose.Schema({
  username: {
    type: String,
    required: true,
  },

 orderId: {
    type: String,
    required: true,
  },

  items: {
    type: [String],
    required: true,
  },
  count: {
    type: Number,
  },
 price: {
    type: String,
  },
  email: {
    type: String,
    required: true,
  },
  address: {
    type: String,
    required: true,
  },
  placed_date: {
    type: Date,
```

```
    default: Date.now,
  },
  status: {
    type: String,
  },
});


module.exports = Order = mongoose.model("order",
OrderSchema);
```

The provided code defines a MongoDB schema using Mongoose for storing orders in the database. The schema includes various fields. Each field specifies its data type and any validation rules.

For example, username and orderId are strings and are required fields, while count is a number. The placed_date field is set to the current date by default if not specified. Once the schema is defined, it is exported as the Order model using mongoose.model(). This model can then be used to interact with the orders collection in the MongoDB database, allowing for operations such as creating, reading, updating, and deleting order documents.

Now, create another folder routes and create a file orders.js inside that. Refer to Code 5.4 and copy it to the new file. We will break down the code below to the code section.

```
Code 5.4 - Server -> routes -> orders.js
const mongoose = require("mongoose");
const express = require("express");
const router = express.Router();
const Order = require("../models/Order");

//Insert Order
router.post("/add", (req, res) => {
```

```
Order.create(req.body)
    .then((order) => res.json({ msg: "Order added
successfully", order }))
    .catch((err) =>

    res.status(400).json({ error: `Unable to add this
order ${err}` })
    );
});

// Get all orders by username
router.get("/user/:username", authenticate, (req, res) =>
{
  const username = req.params.username;
  Order.find({ username: username })
    .then((orders) => {
      if (!orders || orders.length === 0) {
        return res
          .status(404)
          .json({ notFound: "No Orders found for this
user" });
      }
      res.json(orders);
    })
    .catch((err) => res.status(500).json({ error: `Server
Error: ${err}` }));
});

module.exports = router;
```

This code defines routes for handling CRUD operations related to orders.

The POST route /add is responsible for adding a new order to the database. It expects the order data in the request body and uses the Order model's create method to save the order to the database. If the operation is successful, it responds with a success message along with the created order details. If an error occurs, it sends a 400-status code along with an error message.

The GET route /user/:username retrieves all orders associated with a particular user. Like the previous route, it extracts the username from the request parameters and uses the find method of the Order model to retrieve all orders with the specified username from the database. If orders are found, they are returned as a JSON response.

Now, the final step is to create an index.js file directly under server folder. As in the previous step, copy the code section and we can go in depth below. Refer to Code 5.5.

```
Code 5.5 - Server-> index.js
const express = require("express");
const connectDB = require("./db/connection");
const ordersRoutes = require("./routes/orders");
const cors = require("cors");
const bodyParser = require("body-parser");
const path = require("path"); // Import the 'path' module

const app = express();

app.use(cors({ origin: true, credentials: true }));

// use the body-parser  to parse JSON and URL-encoded data
app.use(bodyParser.json());
app.use(bodyParser.urlencoded({ extended: true }));

app.use("/api/orders", ordersRoutes);
```

```
// Connect Database
connectDB();

// Serve static files from the client/build directory
app.use(express.static(path.join(__dirname, '..',
'client', 'build')));

// Define route to serve the client's index.html
app.get('/', (req, res) => {
    res.sendFile(path.join(__dirname, '..', 'client',
'build', 'index.html'));
});

const port = process.env.PORT || 8080;
app.listen(port, () => console.log(`Server running on port
${port}`));
```

This will be the start up file for server. This code sets up an Express server to handle HTTP requests related to orders. Firstly, the code imports required modules such as Express, connection to the database (connectDB), routes for orders, CORS for enabling cross-origin resource sharing, body-parser for parsing JSON and URL-encoded data, and the path module for working with file and directory paths. Then the code initializes an Express application by calling the express() function and assigning it to the variable app.

It sets up middleware using app.use(). CORS middleware is used to allow cross-origin requests. Body-parser middleware is used to parse incoming request bodies in JSON and URL-encoded formats.

It defines routes for handling orders. The /api/orders route is associated with the ordersRoutes module using app.use(). This means that requests with paths starting with /api/orders will be handled by the ordersRoutes module.

Next, it connects to the MongoDB database using the `connectDB()` function. Then, we defined the `express.static` middleware, which is used for serving static files such as HTML, CSS, and JavaScript files. The `path.join(__dirname, '..', 'client', 'build')` is used to construct the absolute path to the client/build directory by joining the current directory (`__dirname`) with the relative path to the client/build directory. Next, we defined route to server `index.html` from the client, that is from React. This ensures that when we run server at `localhost:8080`, it will load the home page of the React app.

Finally, it starts the server to listen for incoming requests on the specified port.

Time to run the app. Ensure you are in the server folder in Terminal and run `npm start`. Now the server will be listening on the port 8080. Refer to Image 5.9 for a visual guide of how the project set up looks like now.

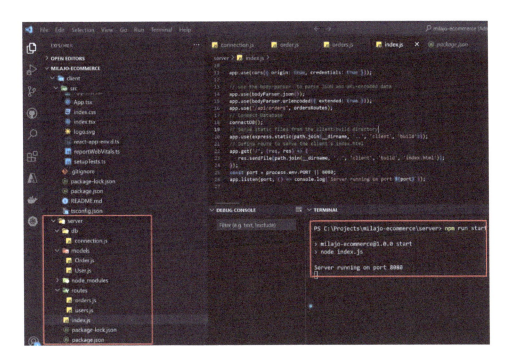

Before we move on to the final two stages on the client side, we can test if the server works as expected. Keep the local server running and go to Extensions in VS Code and install an extension called ThunderClient. This will help us to test the API calls.

Click on ThunderClient from the left App bar and click on New Request. Select POST method. Enter http://localhost:8080/api/orders/add in the URL. In the body section, enter a test order data. The one I used, is below:

```
{
    "username": "globalUser",
    "orderId": "MJ65965",
    "items": ["Diamond Ring", "Ferragamo BOXYZ bag"],
    "count": 2,
    "price":"$966.50",
    "email": "example@example.com",
    "address": "11 React Street, React Cafe, Melbourne",
    "status": "Confirmed"
}
```

You will receive a message saying Order added successfully. Refer to Image 5.10, where steps highlighted.

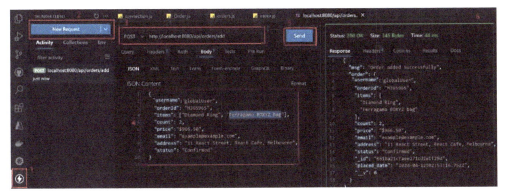

Image 5.10: Adding an order.

This way, you can add multiple orders for testing purposes. Now if you go back to your MongoDB dashboard at https://cloud.mongodb.com/ -> Database -> Explore collections, you can see that the orders are stored in the order collection. Apply filter in the collection using {"username":"globalUser"}. You can view the created orders of the globalUser. Refer to Image 5.11 for my example.

Image 5.11: order collection

This way you can test retrieve the orders specific to a user using username. Refer to Image 5.12, where I queried my orders using username. I had created two orders with the same username.

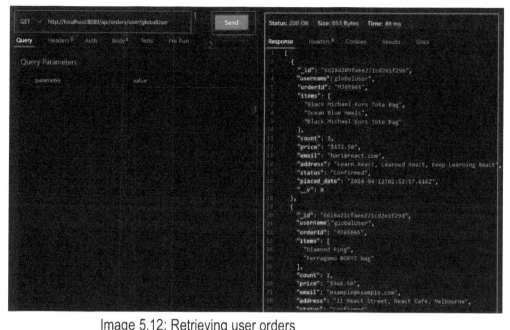

Image 5.12: Retrieving user orders

Now that we've successfully tested both the endpoints for saving and retrieving orders, it's time to proceed to the next stage of our development process. In this stage, we'll focus on further enhancing our React application to enable the functionality for saving an order.

Stage 3: Save Orders

Let's head back to our React code and improve the Trolley component to prepare an order object. Once we've structured the order object, we'll send an API request to the server, enabling the storage of the order in the database's order collection. To achieve this, we'll update the `andlePlaceOrder` function in the Trolley component. Simply navigate to the `Trolley.tsx` file and replace the existing `handlePlaceOrder` function with the code provided in Code 5.6.

Code 5.6 Trolley.tsx - handlePlaceOrder function
```
const handlePlaceOrder = () => {
    const username = 'globalUser'; // Hardcoded user name
    const orderId = 'MJ' + Math.floor(10000 +
Math.random() * 90000); // Random order ID starting with
'MJ'
    const items = trolleyItems.map(item => `${item.title}
x ${item.quantity}`); // Extracting item title and
quantities from trolley items
    const count = trolleyItems.reduce((total, item) =>
total + item.quantity, 0); // Total quantity of items in
the trolley
    const status = 'confirmed'; // Hardcoded status

    // Construct the order object
    const order = {
      username,
      orderId,

    items,
      count,
      price,
      email,
```

```
      address,
      status
  };

  // Send a POST request to add the order
  fetch('/api/orders/add', {
    method: 'POST',
    headers: {
      'Content-Type': 'application/json'
    },
    body: JSON.stringify(order)
  })
    .then(response => response.json())
    .then(data => {
      console.log('Order added successfully:', data);
      setOpenSuccessSnackbar(true);
    })
    .catch(error => {
      console.error('Error adding order:', error);
    });
};
```

This function will be triggered when the user clicks on a button to place an order. Inside this function, it generates a unique order ID starting with MJ and followed by five random digits. Then, it constructs an order object containing details such as user ID, order ID, items in the trolley along with their quantities, total count of items, price, email, address, and status of the order. After constructing the order object, it sends a POST request to the specific endpoint (/api/orders/add) with the order data in JSON format. If the request is successful, it displays a success message to the user, indicating that the order has been placed successfully.

Note that we have temporarily hardcoded the username in this implementation. However, we will replace it with the actual username once we implement the authentication functionality in the upcoming chapter.

Now, let's shift our focus to testing the endpoint directly from the application. Begin by navigating to the terminal and ensuring that you are within the server folder. Then, execute the command npm build-start. This command will first build the client and then start the server. After initiating the build process by running this command, keep an eye out for the message Server running on port 8080 to confirm that the build is complete and the server is operational.

Once done, open your browser and visit http://localhost:8080. Proceed to add a few items with varying quantities to your trolley and place the order. After that, head to https://cloud.mongodb.com, log in, and filter the collection with the username globalUser. Here, you'll find the details of the placed order. This successful implementation demonstrates the interaction between the client, server, and database in saving orders. Now, let's proceed to retrieve the orders and display them on the My Orders page.

Stage 4: Retrieve Orders

Now, it is time to design our MyOrders component, so that users can view their orders in a user-friendly view. To start with, create a CSS module MyOrders.module.css under the folder styles, and copy the code from section Code 5.7.

Code 5.7 MyOrders.module.css
```
.container {
  margin: 20px;
}
.title {
```

```css
    margin-bottom: 20px !important;
}
.list {
  width: 100%;
  padding-top: 10px;
}
.listItem {
  border: 1px solid #ccc;

 margin-bottom: 10px;
  padding: 10px;
}
.emptyMessage {
  margin-top: 20px;
}
.card {
  margin-bottom: 20px;
  border: 1px solid #d3d3d3;
}
.address {
  padding-top: 5px;
  color: #666;
}
.header {
  color: #ff5733;
  cursor: pointer;
}
.status {
  padding-bottom: 5px;
  color: green;
}
.items {
  padding-top: 5px;
  color: #666;
```

```
}
.orderIcon {
  color: #2596be;
  font-size: 30px !important;
}
```

Now, use the code from Code 5.8 and replace the existing template code in
MyOrders.tsx. let me explain the code below to that.

Code 5.8 - MyOrders.tsx
```
import { useState, useEffect } from 'react';
import { Card, CardContent, Typography, List, ListItem,
ListItemText, Divider, ListItemIcon, Collapse } from
'@mui/material';
import { ExpandMore, ExpandLess, PlaylistAddCheck } from
'@mui/icons-material';
import styles from '../styles/MyOrders.module.css';

interface Order {
  orderId: string;
  status: string;
  count: number;
  items: string[];
  address: string;
}

const MyOrders = () => {
  const [orders, setOrders] = useState<Order[]>([]);
  const [expanded, setExpanded] = useState<string[]>([]);

  useEffect(() => {
    // Fetch orders specific to the user with id
'globalUser'
```

```
const fetchOrders = async () => {

    try {
        const response = await
fetch(`/api/orders/user/globalUser`);
        if (response.ok) {
            const data = await response.json();
            setOrders(data);

        } else {
            console.error('Failed to fetch orders:',
response.statusText);
        }
    } catch (error) {
        console.error('Error fetching orders:', error);
    }
};

    fetchOrders();
  }, []);

  const handleExpand = (orderId: string) => {
    setExpanded(expanded.includes(orderId) ?
expanded.filter(id => id !== orderId) : [...expanded,
orderId]);
  };

  return (
    <div className={styles.container}>
      <Typography variant="h4" className={styles.title}>
        My Orders
      </Typography>

{orders.length > 0 ? (
```

```jsx
<List className={styles.list}>
  {orders.map((order) => (
    <Card key={order.orderId}
className={styles.card}>
      <ListItem onClick={() =>
handleExpand(order.orderId)}>
        <ListItemIcon >
          <PlaylistAddCheck
className={styles.orderIcon} />
        </ListItemIcon>
        <ListItemText className={styles.header}
primary={`Order ID: ${order.orderId}`} />
        {expanded.includes(order.orderId) ?
<ExpandLess /> : <ExpandMore />}
      </ListItem>
      <Collapse
in={expanded.includes(order.orderId)} timeout="auto"
unmountOnExit>
        <CardContent>
          <Typography color="textSecondary"
gutterBottom className={styles.status}>
            Status: {order.status}
          </Typography>
          <Divider />
          <Typography variant="body1"
component="p" className={styles.items}>
            Items ({order.count}):
          </Typography>
          <List>

          {order.items.map((item, index) => (
            <ListItem key={index}>
              <ListItemText primary={item} />
            </ListItem>
```

```
                ))}
              </List>
              <Divider />
              <Typography variant="body2"
component="p" className={styles.address}>
                  The order will be shipped to:
{order.address}
              </Typography>
            </CardContent>
          </Collapse>
        </Card>
      ))}
    </List>
  ) : (
      <Typography variant="body1"
className={styles.emptyMessage}>
        No orders found.
      </Typography>
    )}
    </div>
  );
};

export default MyOrders;
```

Let's go through the code:

The component imports necessary modules from Material-UI and defines a functional component called MyOrders. It initializes state variables using the useState hook: orders to store fetched orders data and expanded to manage the expanded state of each order.

Upon component mounting, it sends a GET request to the server endpoint `/api/orders/user/globalUser` to retrieve orders specific to the user with username `globalUser`.

If the request is successful, the fetched data is stored in the `orders` state. Like we did for adding an order, this API call establishes the communication between client-server and database.

Each order is rendered within a `Card` component. The `handleExpand` function toggles the expansion state of an order when clicked. If an order is expanded, its ID is added to the expanded state; otherwise, it is removed.

For each order, a `listItem` displays the order ID along with an icon indicating an order. Clicking on an order toggles its expansion state, and the Collapse component conditionally renders the order details (status, items, and shipping address) based on the `expanded` state.

The component applies styles defined in the CSS module (`MyOrders.module.css`) to customize the appearance of various elements such as the container, title, list, card, header, status, items, address, and empty message.

To summarize, this component effectively manages the display of user orders, allowing a user to expand and collapse individual orders to view their details conveniently.

Go back to the terminal and navigate to the `server` folder. Run the command `npm run build-start`. Once the build is complete and server is up and running, open your browser and go to `http://localhost:8080`. Visit My Orders from the top navigation, where you'll find all the orders for the `globalUser`. By default, all orders will be expanded, displaying their details. You can click on each order to collapse or expand it individually. You can refer to Image 5.13 for a visual example.

Image 5.13: My orders (globalUser)

This completes our Manage order process. We have successfully implemented a MERN stack solution for our orders.

Sip

In this chapter, we took our initial steps into the world of MERN stack development, which comprises MongoDB, Express.js, React.js, and Node.js. Our main objective was to implement the My Orders feature within our application. We began by laying the groundwork, setting up a MongoDB database and configuring a dedicated collection to house our orders. Just like a well-brewed cup of coffee requires the perfect blend of beans, water, and temperature, our project required a harmonious integration of server-side and client-side technologies.

With our server-side environment established using Node.js and Express, we ensured smooth interaction between the server and the database. We meticulously tested our API endpoints using the VS Code ThunderClient extension, ensuring our backend operations were running smoothly.

Transitioning back to the client-side code, we enhanced the Trolley component to enable users to place orders effortlessly. This involved orchestrating a call to the server, invoking the order route, and orchestrating the creation of order entries in the database. Moreover, we ensured seamless retrieval of past orders from the server and displayed them on the My Orders page.

As we conclude this chapter, you've refined your full-stack development skills and deepened your understanding of crafting dynamic web applications with React, delving into the intricacies of the MERN stack. Throughout our journey, we relied on a hardcoded test user to simulate real-world scenarios, with plans to implement a user-specific order system in the next chapter, where we'll delve into authentication and display user specific content.

CHAPTER 6

The Passport

Cup

In this final chapter, we continue our journey through the world of MERN stack development, delving into the user authentication. Building upon the foundation laid in the previous chapter, where we focused on managing orders and establishing seamless communication with MongoDB, we now turn our attention to the crucial aspects of user management. Our focus shifts towards implementing authentication mechanisms, enabling users to securely sign up, log in, and access user specific content within our application.

By leveraging the power of passport.js, a versatile authentication middleware for Node.js, we ensure robust user authentication and authorization against our MongoDB database. Additionally, we'll explore how to link users to their respective orders, providing a personalized experience tailored to each user's preferences.

Finally, we'll round off our user management system by implementing a log-out functionality, ensuring users have full control over their session's security. Finally, By the end of this chapter, you will learn to fortify your MERN stack application with layers of security and user-centric features.

Sign Up

Let's begin by establishing a Sign-Up system, enabling users to register using their name, username, and password. We'll break down this process into three stages:

1) Stage 1 (MongoDB): Establishing a User collection in the MongoDB database to store user information securely.

2) Stage 2 (Node.js): Implementing a user route in the Node.js server and integrating authentication mechanisms using Passport.js to ensure secure user registration. Additionally, enable authentication & authorization for order placement and retrieval.

3) Stage 3 (React): Developing the Login component in React and configuring it to interact with the database through the server, enabling seamless communication and user registration flow. Additionally, integrate authentication for order placement and retrieval.

Stage 1: Establishing a User collection in the MongoDB database.

Go to https://cloud.mongodb.com/ and create a new database collection called users. For details, refer to Chapter 5 - section Stage 1: Database Setup with MongoDB - Image 5.7. Also refer Image 6.1

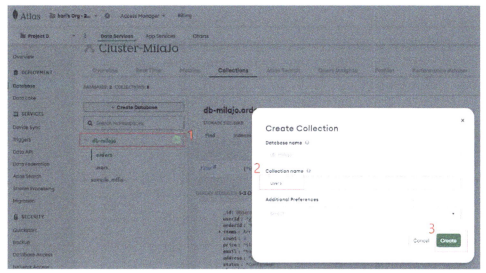

Image 6.1 Create user collection.

That's all for stage 1. Let's move on to complete server-side coding.

Stage 2: Set up user routes and authentication on the server.

For easier comprehension, let's proceed with a detailed, step-by-step approach.

Step 2.1: Develop the User Model

First, we establish the core structure for managing user data within our application by creating a User model. This model will define the schema for user documents in our MongoDB database, including essential fields such as username, password, name, email, and address. This is a critical foundational step for securely handling user information.

Step 2.2: Configure Passport for User Authentication

Next, we integrate Passport.js, a widely used authentication middleware for Node.js. This tool will enable us to authenticate users based on various strategies, including the straightforward username and password method. In our setup, Passport.js will authenticate users against the credentials stored in the MongoDB user's collection, ensuring that only authorized users can engage with the application.

Step 2.3: Establish Routes for User Authentication

We will then proceed to set up specific routes to handle user authentication processes such as sign-up, login, and logout. Like our approach with order management, we'll create a new file within the routes folder. This file will host all the necessary endpoints for managing user interactions.

Step 2.4: Enhance Session Management and Authentication

Following the route setup, we'll focus on incorporating and configuring vital middleware components essential for robust session management and secure user authentication.

Step 2.5: Secure Order Routes with Authentication

The final step involves tightening the security around our order management routes. We'll add authentication checks to order routes to ensure they are accessible only by authenticated users, thereby enhancing the security and integrity of order operations within the system.

Step 2.1: Develop the User model

In this step, we're setting up the foundation for securely managing user data in our application. We'll create a user model that defines the structure of user documents in our MongoDB database. This model includes fields such as username, password, name, email, and address.

This is like how we defined an Order model earlier. However, in this case, we're adding extra functionality to handle user authentication securely.

To get started, create a new file named User.js within the Server -> Models folder. Then, paste the provided code snippet from Code 6.1 into this new file. I'll explain the code in more detail below to the code section.

Code 6.1- Server -> Models -> User.js

```
const mongoose = require("mongoose");
const bcrypt = require("bcrypt");
mongoose.promise = Promise;
const UserSchema = new mongoose.Schema({
  username: {
    type: String,
    required: true,
  },
  password: {
    type: String,
    required: true,
  },
```

```
  name: {

   type: String,
    required: true,
  },
  email: {
    type: String,
    required: true,
  },
  address: {
    type: String,
    required: true,
  },
});
UserSchema.methods = {
  checkPassword: function (inputPassword) {
    return bcrypt.compareSync(inputPassword,
this.password);
  },
  hashPassword: (plainTextPassword) => {
    return bcrypt.hashSync(plainTextPassword, 10);
  },
};

UserSchema.pre("save", function (next) {
  if (!this.password) {
    console.log("No password provided");
    next();
  } else {
    this.password = this.hashPassword(this.password);
    console.log("Password hashed.");
    next();
  }
```

```
});

module.exports = User = mongoose.model("User",
UserSchema);
```

The code requires two libraries: mongoose for interacting with MongoDB and bcrypt for hashing passwords securely. The UserSchema defines the structure of a user document in the database. It includes fields like username, password, name etc. each with a specified data type and whether it's required.

The checkPassword method compares a plaintext password (input by a user during login) with the hashed password stored in the database. It uses bcrypt.compareSync to perform a secure comparison.

The hashPassword method takes a plaintext password and returns its hashed version. It uses bcrypt.hashSync to hash the password with a specified strength (10 rounds of hashing).

The Pre-save Hook is a middleware function that runs before saving a user document to the database. It checks if the user document has a password field. If it does, it hashes the password using the hashPassword method before saving it to the database.

Finally, the User model is created using mongoose.model, which takes two arguments: the name of the model (User) and the schema (UserSchema). This model represents the collection of users in the MongoDB database.

In this step, to ensure that passwords are stored securely, we employed techniques for hashing and checking passwords. This adds an extra layer of protection to user accounts, making it more difficult for unauthorized access to occur.

Step 2.2: Configure Passport for User Authentication

Passport.js is a popular authentication middleware for Node.js applications. It provides a simple and flexible way to authenticate users using different strategies, such as username and password, OAuth authentication with providers like Google, Facebook, and many others. In our scenario, Passport.js will be configured to authenticate users against the username and password stored in the users collection in MongoDB, ensuring that only authorized users can sign up and access the application's features.

Create a new file named passport.js under Server folder. Then, paste the provided code snippet from section 6.2 into this new file. I'll explain the code in more detail below to the code section.

Code 6.2 Server-> passport.js

```
const passport = require("passport");
const LocalStrategy = require("passport-local").Strategy;
const User = require("./models/User");

// called on login, saves the id to session
req.session.passport.user = {id:'..'}

passport.serializeUser(async (user, done) => {
  console.log(user);
  done(null, { _id: user._id });
});

// user object attaches to the request as req.user
passport.deserializeUser(async (id, done) => {
  try {
    const user = await User.findOne({ _id: id },
"username");
```

```javascript
    console.log(user);
    done(null, user);
  } catch (err) {
    done(err);
  }
});

const strategy = new LocalStrategy(
  { usernameField: "username" },
  async function (username, password, done) {
    try {
      const user = await User.findOne({ username: username
});
      if (!user) {
        return done(null, false, { error: "Incorrect
username" });
      }
      if (!user.checkPassword(password)) {
        return done(null, false, { error: "Incorrect
password" });
      }

   return done(null, user);
    } catch (err) {
      return done(err);
    }
  }
);

passport.use(strategy);

module.exports = passport;
```

Firstly, we import the Passport library which we had installed during the server set up in Chapter 5 (Refer to Code 5.1 and explanation). Next, we imported the LocalStrategy constructor from Passport, which is used for username and password-based authentication. Then, we imported the User model which we defined earlier in Code 6.1.

The passport.serializeUser function is called when a user logs in, and it saves the user's ID to the session. It's used to determine what data should be stored in the session.

The passport.deserializeUser function serves to retrieve a user's data from the session storage based on user's ID. In our application's context, when a user requests access to protected resources or performs actions like placing an order or fetching order history, the server first verifies the user's authentication status. If the user is authenticated and has an active session, Passport employs the deserializeUser function to fetch their data from the session. It's important to note that we haven't yet secured the endpoints for order-related actions, but we plan to address this in the final stage.
The _id field in a MongoDB database is automatically generated as a unique identifier for each document in a collection. When a new user document is created and saved to the database, MongoDB automatically generates a unique _id value for that document. This _id value is usually a 12-byte hexadecimal string that is globally unique across the entire database.

In the context of the Passport authentication system shown in the code, the user._id refers to the unique identifier of the user document in the database. This _id value is used to serialize the user data into the session and later deserialize it to retrieve the user data when needed.

The line of code, `const strategy = new LocalStrategy(...)` creates a new instance of `LocalStrategy`, which defines how Passport will authenticate users based on their username and password. It takes an options object as its first argument, which specifies the name of the username field in the request.

The second argument is an asynchronous function that defines the authentication logic. Inside this function, a user is looked up in the database based on the provided username. If the user exists, their password is checked against the provided password using the `checkPassword` method. We have defined this method in the User mode. If the password matches, the user object is passed to the done callback to indicate successful authentication.

The line `passport.use(strategy)` tells Passport to use the defined local authentication strategy for authenticating users.

Finally, we export the configured Passport instance, which can then be imported and used in other parts of the application to handle authentication.

To sum up, this code sets up Passport for user authentication using a local strategy (username and password). It defines how user data is serialized and deserialized, configures the local authentication strategy, and exports the configured Passport instance for use in other parts of the application.

Step 2.3: Establish Routes for User Authentication

To facilitate user sign-up, login, and logout functionalities, we'll define routes within our server application. Like how we handled orders, we'll create a new file named `users.js` within the `routes` folder of our `server` directory.

Once the file is created, we'll add three route methods: one for signing up users, another for user login, and a third for user logout. Additionally, we'll include logic to ensure that a user is not signed up multiple times.

After creating the users.js file, copy and paste the provided code snippet from section 6.3 into this new file. I'll provide a detailed explanation of the code following that.

Code 6.3 Server-> routes -> users.js

```
const express = require("express");
const router = express.Router();
const User = require("../models/User");
const passport = require("../passport");

const isSignedUp = async (req, res, next) => {
  const { username } = req.body;
  try {
    const registered = await User.findOne({ username });
    if (registered) {
      res.json({
        error: `A user already exists with the username:
${username}`,
      });
      return;
    }
    next();
  } catch (error) {
    console.error(error);

    res.status(500).json({ error: "Internal server error"
});
  }
```

```
};

const signUpUser = async (req, res, next) => {
  const { username, password, name, email, address } =
req.body;
  try {
    const newUser = new User({
      username,
      password: password,
      name: name,
      email: email,
      address: address,
    });
    await newUser.save();
    res
      .status(201)
      .json({ success: "Signed up successfully, you can
now login." });
  } catch (error) {
    console.error(error);
    res.status(500).json({ error: "Internal server error"
});
  }
};

const login = (req, res) => {
  req.login(req.user, function (err) {
    if (err) {
      res.json({ error: err });

    }
    req.session.username = req.user.username;
    const userToReturn = { ...req.user._doc }; // Copy
user details
```

```
    delete userToReturn.password; // Remove password from
the details sent to client
    return res.send(userToReturn);
  });
};

const logout = (req, res) => {
  req.logout(function (err) {
    if (err) {
      return res.send({ error: "no user to log out" });
    }
    res.send({ success: "logged out" });
  });
};

router.post("/signup", isSignedUp, signUpUser);

router.post("/login", passport.authenticate("local"),
login);

router.post("/logout", logout);

module.exports = router;
```

The code begins by importing necessary dependencies like Express, the user model, and the passport configuration.

The isSignedUp function is defined to check if a user with the provided username already exists in the database. If the user is already registered, it sends back an error response indicating that the username is already taken. If not, it passes control to the next middleware function.

The `signUpUser` function handles the sign-up process. It extracts user data from the request body, creates a new user instance with the provided details, and saves it to the database. Upon successful registration, it sends a success response indicating that the user has been signed up.

The `login` function is defined to handle user login attempts. It utilizes Passport's local authentication strategy to authenticate users based on their username and password. When a user attempts to log in, this function is triggered after their credentials have been verified. The `req.login()` method, provided by Passport.js, is used to establish a login session. If there are no errors, it proceeds to store the user's username in the session for later use, which helps in identifying the user in subsequent requests.

Additionally, it prepares a user object by copying user details and removing sensitive information like the password to ensure security. Finally, it sends this cleaned user object back to the client. This method effectively handles the login process, sets up a session for the user, and ensures that sensitive data like passwords are not sent back to the client, enhancing security.

The `logout` function is responsible for logging out users. When invoked, it calls the `req.logout` function provided by Passport to remove the user's session. If successful, it sends a success response indicating that the user has been logged out.

Finally, the router instance containing all the defined routes is exported to be used in other parts of the application. In short, this code sets up routes for user sign-up, login, and logout, ensuring that new users can register, existing users can log in securely, and users can log out of their accounts when needed.

Step 2.4: Enhance Session management and Authentication

The next step in our server setup is to update the `index.js` file, which serves as the main entry point for our server. The focus of these modifications is to incorporate and configure critical middleware components that are essential for session management and secure user authentication.

To proceed, you will need to replace the existing `index.js` file in the server directory with the new code provided in section 6.4. This updated code will integrate advanced functionalities into our server's core infrastructure, enabling it to manage user sessions and authenticate identities more effectively.

After making these changes, I will provide a detailed breakdown of how these updates enhance our server's capabilities and the specific roles of the newly integrated components.

Code 6.4 - Server -> index.js

```
const express = require("express");
const connectDB = require("./db/connection");
const ordersRoutes = require("./routes/orders");
const cors = require("cors");
const bodyParser = require("body-parser");
const path = require("path"); // Import the 'path' module


//Changes-1 start (from Chapter 5, Code 5.5)
const usersRoutes = require("./routes/users");
const session = require("express-session");
const MongoStore = require("connect-mongo");
const passport = require("./passport");
require("dotenv").config();
//Changes-1 end (from Chapter 5, Code 5.5)
```

```
const app = express();

app.use(cors({ origin: true, credentials: true }));

// use the body-parser  to parse JSON and URL-encoded data
app.use(bodyParser.json());
app.use(bodyParser.urlencoded({ extended: true }));

// Connect Database
connectDB();

//Changes-2 start (from Chapter 5, Code 5.5)
app.use(
  session({
    secret: "RX7b#P2$rLz5@TqY&9FvG3*sCAFE",
    resave: false,
    saveUninitialized: false,
    store: MongoStore.create({ mongoUrl:
process.env.CONN_STRING }),
  })
);

app.use(passport.initialize());
app.use(passport.session());

app.use("/api/users", usersRoutes);
//Changes-2 end (from Chapter 5, Code 5.5)

app.use("/api/orders", ordersRoutes);

// Serve static files from the client/build directory
app.use(express.static(path.join(__dirname, "..",
"client", "build")));
```

```
// Define route to serve the client's index.html
app.get("/", (req, res) => {
  res.sendFile(path.join(__dirname, "..", "client",
"build", "index.html"));
});

const port = process.env.PORT || 8080;
app.listen(port, () =>

  console.log(`Server running on port
${process.env.PORT}`)
);
```

Let's take a closer look at the above updates we've made to the index.js file to enhance user management and security features. These updates are detailed in the code, with comments marking the start and end of each section. For reference to the index.js before these changes, see Chapter 5, Code section 5.5.

Changes-1: Importing Modules and Configurations

We started by importing usersRoutes from a specific directory, which contains predefined paths that manage user interactions like logging in and signing up. Following this, we brought in the express-session module, essential for managing sessions. A session is like a unique ID card given to a user when they interact with our application. It helps the server remember the user across multiple pages or actions, which is crucial for functionalities like keeping a user logged in as they browse.

We also introduced MongoStore, which utilizes MongoDB to save these session IDs. This is an upgrade from storing session information temporarily in server memory because it means user sessions can be remembered even if the server needs to restart, ensuring users don't get logged out unexpectedly.

Furthermore, we included the passport module, crucial for verifying a user's identity during login processes, and dotenv, which allows our application to securely access sensitive settings stored in our environment file without hard coding them into our source code.

Changes-2: Configuring Middleware

This section involves setting up middleware, which are tools that help handle requests and data more efficiently before they reach the core logic of our application or after they leave it.

We configured session middleware with several security settings:

secret: A secret key used to sign the session ID cookie, which helps prevent the session data from being tampered with. You can use any complex string for this.

resave: Set to false, this tells our application not to save session data back to the database unless it has been changed, which saves resources.

saveUninitialized: Also set to false, prevents new sessions that haven't been modified from being saved, which enhances security and efficiency.

Store: This is configured with MongoStore.create, it directs the session middleware to use MongoDB to store session data. The MongoDB connection string is retrieved from environment variables.

We also initialized `passport` to handle user authentication and set up `passport.session()` to maintain login sessions. It works together with the express session middleware to manage user sessions across multiple requests.

Finally, we directed the server to use `usersRoutes` for handling all user-related actions under the `/api/users` endpoint. This setup is analogous to how we manage order-related actions, ensuring consistency and structure in our application.

By making these updates, we've significantly enhanced our application's backend to manage user sessions and authentication securely and efficiently. This infrastructure is essential for any web application that requires reliable user account management and session handling capabilities.

Before we proceed to the final step of our server configuration, let's conduct a test on the Signup endpoint to ensure it's functioning correctly. Here's how to do it:

1. Start the server by running npm `start` from your command line.

2. Open Visual Studio Code and access the `ThunderClient` extension.

3. Configure `ThunderClient` to use the endpoint `http://localhost:8080/api/users/signup`.

4. In the request body, input the following JSON data:

```
{
    "username": "cafeuser",
    "password": "cafepassword",
    "name": "Cafe User",
```

```
        "email": "cafeuser@reactcafe.com",
        "address": "564 React Street, Mern City"
    }
```

5. Send the request. You should receive a response indicating `Signed up successfully, you can now login.`

For a visual reference to this test steps and the successful response, refer to Image 6.2.

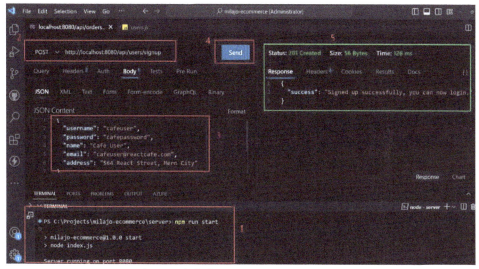

Image 6.2: Signup a user

After testing the Signup endpoint, you can verify that the new user has been successfully created by following these steps:

1. Go to cloud.mongodb.com and log in with your credentials.
2. Navigate to the 'collections' section to view the data.

3. Look for the 'users' collection and open it to check for the newly added user information.

You should be able to see the entry for the new user as shown in Image 6.3. This confirms that the Signup process not only responds appropriately but also effectively creates new user records in the database.

Image 6.3 New user record in user collection

This will confirm that our Signup endpoint is operational and ready to handle new user registrations.

If you attempt to sign up with the same user again, the system will notify you that the user already exists, preventing duplicate user records from being created.

Next, let's create another user account with the username globalUser. This step is necessary for us to effectively test order authorization in subsequent parts of our setup. You can use any test data for the other attributes such as the password, email, and address.

You might remember that we previously used the username globalUser before we implemented user-specific orders. As a result, there is already some order data associated with this user in the database. This existing data will be useful for testing how our system manages order access under the new user-specific configurations.

Additionally, when you use the login endpoint with the username and password, you should receive an Ok response, indicating successful authentication. During this process, you will also see that the user object is retrieved without the password for security reasons, and you can observe the unique _id assigned to the user, which is a unique identifier generated by MongoDB. For visual steps of these operations, you can refer to Image 6.4.

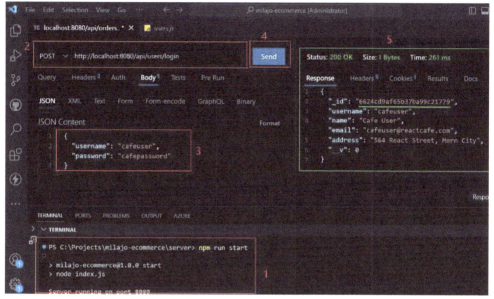

Image 6.4 User login

Similarly, if you provide an incorrect password here, you will receive an unauthorized error. This ensures that only users with the correct credentials can access the system. You can try this out.

Step 2.5: Secure Order Routes with Authentication

The final update in setting up our server involves enhancing the security of our order management system by updating the orders.js file. This file handles all routes related to order operations, such as adding and retrieving orders. We will be integrating authentication checks to ensure that these operations are protected and can only be accessed by authenticated users.

To implement these changes, replace the existing orders.js file in the router folder of your server directory with the updated code from section 6.5. I will provide an explanation of these modifications once they are in place. Here is an overview of the changes included in the updated orders.js:

Code 6.5 - Server -> routes -> orders.js

```
const express = require('express');
const router = express.Router();
const Order = require("../models/Order")

// Middleware to protect routes with Passport
authentication & authorization
const authenticate = (req, res, next) => {
  if (!req.isAuthenticated()) {

    return res.status(401).json({ error: "Unauthorized
access" });
  }
  const { username } = req.params; // This captures the
username from the route parameter

  if (req.session.username !== username) {
    return res
      .status(403)
```

```javascript
      .json({ error: "Access denied: You can only access
your own orders" });
  }

  next(); // Proceed if authenticated and authorized
};
//Insert Order
router.post('/add', authenticate, (req, res) => {
  Order.create(req.body)
    .then(order => res.json({ msg: 'Order added
successfully', order }))
    .catch(err => res.status(400).json({ error: `Unable to
add this order ${err}` }));
});
// Get all orders by username
router.get("/user/:username", authenticate, (req, res) =>
{
  const username = req.params.username;
  Order.find({ username: username })
    .then((orders) => {
      if (!orders || orders.length === 0) {
        return res

      .status(404)
        .json({ notFound: "No Orders found for this
user" });
      }
      res.json(orders);
    })
    .catch((err) => res.status(500).json({ error: `Server
Error: ${err}` }));
});
module.exports = router;
```

In this updated code, we've introduced a function named `authenticate`. This function utilizes the `req.isAuthenticated()` method provided by Passport.js to check if the user making a request is currently authenticated— essentially verifying if the user's session contains valid login information. If the user is not authenticated, the function halts the process and returns an `Unauthorized access` message.

`const { username } = req.params;` destructures the username from `req.params`, which contains route parameters. This is used to get the username from the URL. After confirming the user is authenticated, this line checks if the username stored in the session matches the username in the URL. The username is stored in the session when the user logged in, refer to Step 3: Setting up Routes for User Authentication. If they do not match, it sends a 403 Forbidden HTTP response with a JSON message saying `Access denied: You can only access your own orders`. This ensures users can only access resources that belong to them and not to others.

This middleware effectively protects sensitive routes by ensuring that only logged-in users can access them, and even then, only their own data based on their username. This is crucial for maintaining data security and user privacy in applications that handle user-specific data.

Both the endpoint for adding a new order and the endpoint for retrieving orders by user ID are now secured using this authenticate function. It is added as middleware to each route, ensuring that only authenticated users can perform these operations. This security measure protects sensitive user data and ensures that order transactions are conducted securely within our application.

Recall our previous session where we tested the endpoint for retrieving orders using the `ThunderClient` extension in Visual Studio Code, as documented in Chapter 5, Stage 2 – Server Configuration, and shown in Image 5.11. With the recent security updates implemented, these endpoints now require the user to be logged in.

To test the updated functionality, start the server by running npm `start` from your command line. Once the server is up, attempt to retrieve orders for `globalUser` using ThunderClient as before. You'll notice that unlike our previous tests, you will now encounter an Unauthorized error. This is expected behavior as the order endpoints are now secured with authentication, preventing unauthorized access. This demonstrates the effectiveness of our new security measures. For a visual reference to this test and the error response, refer to Image 6.5, which illustrates this.

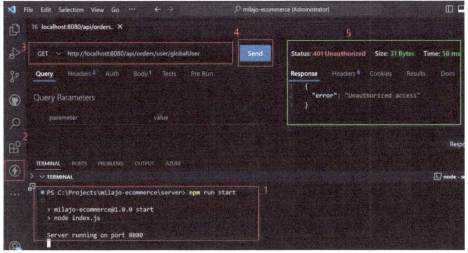

Image 6.5: Retreive orders (protected)

Before implementing the security updates in orders.js, if you tried executing the same request to retrieve orders using ThunderClient, you would find that it gets executed just as before, without any restriction. This observation highlights the necessity and impact of the security enhancements we've introduced to protect sensitive endpoints.

I encourage you to log in using the `cafeuser` account, following the steps outlined previously in the last step. For guidance, refer to Image 6.4. Once you're logged in, try accessing the orders endpoint to get the orders of `globalUser` again. This time, you'll receive an error message stating, `Access denied: You can only access your own orders`. This occurs because you are logged in as `cafeuser` but attempting to access orders associated with `globalUser`.

Next, proceed to log out using the logout endpoint. After logging out, sign in again, this time using the `globalUser` account. Now, when you try to access the orders for `globalUser`, you should be able to retrieve the data successfully, since the user is correctly authenticated and authorized. This process effectively demonstrates the robust authentication and authorization mechanisms of our secure system.

With the server-side authentication setup now complete, we'll turn our attention to the client side of our application. Next up, we're heading back into the world of React to develop a Login component. We'll leverage the endpoints we've already tested to ensure that the front-end functionality aligns smoothly with our established backend services.

Stage 3: Developing the Login Functionality

To ensure a thorough and comprehensible setup, let's break down this final stage into several manageable steps:

Step 3.1 Set Up Authentication Context

The initial step is to create an authentication provider component to handle authentication state using React Context. This step is critical as it lays the groundwork for a scalable and maintainable way to manage user sessions across the application.

Step 3.2: Construct the Login Component

Next task is to create a Login component that includes both login and signup functionalities. This component will serve as the interface for user authentication, interacting directly with MongoDB via the server.

Step 3.3: Enhance Routes and Navigation

The next step involves updating the application's routing to incorporate the new Login component. Additionally, the navigation bar will be modified to include a Logout button. This ensures that users can conveniently log out from any page on the website.

Step 3.4: Revise Trolley and My Orders Components

The final step is to modify the Trolley and My Orders components. These updates will enable the system to save and retrieve orders specific to the logged-in user, moving away from the previous approach of using a global user for all orders. This change enhances personalized user interaction and security within the application.

Step 3.1: Set Up Authentication Context

This component establishes an essential foundation for managing user authentication states throughout our React application by using Context API. This setup includes creating two contexts: AuthContext and AuthDispatchContext, which help in accessing and updating the authentication state from any component within our application.

Create a new component AuthProvider.tsx under the components folder. Copy the code from Code 6.6, and let me explain the implementation below to that.

Code 6.6 – Client -> src -> components -> AuthProvider.tsx

```
import { createContext, Dispatch, SetStateAction,
useState, ReactNode } from "react";

export const AuthContext = createContext<string>('');
export const AuthDispatchContext =
createContext<Dispatch<SetStateAction<string>> |
undefined>(undefined);

function AuthProvider(props: { children: ReactNode }) {
  const { children } = props;
  const [loggedInUser, setLoggedInUser] = useState('');


  return (
    <AuthContext.Provider value={loggedInUser}>
      <AuthDispatchContext.Provider
value={setLoggedInUser}>
        {children}
      </AuthDispatchContext.Provider>
    </AuthContext.Provider>
```

```
    );
};
export default AuthProvider;
```

AuthContext is created to store the current state of the logged-in user, initially set to an empty string, indicating no user is logged in. This context allows any component in your application to access the username of the logged-in user directly, facilitating features that require knowledge of the current user. AuthDispatchContext provides a way for components to update the logged-in user's state. It accept a function (setLoggedInUser) that updates the state.

The AuthProvider component wraps the provided children with both the AuthContext.Provider and the AuthDispatchContext.Provider. This arrangement allows any child components in the app to consume and modify the authentication state as needed.

The AuthProvider uses the useState hook to maintain the loggedInUser state, which tracks who is currently logged in. The setLoggedInUser function from this hook is provided to AuthDispatchContext, enabling child components to update the logged-in user's state easily.

By wrapping the relevant parts of our app with the AuthProvider, we make the loggedInUser state and the setLoggedInUser function available throughout your component tree. This setup is crucial for maintaining a coherent state related to user authentication.

Let's move on to build the login component!

Step 3.2: Construct the Login Component

The Login component in our application serves as the interface where users can either sign in to their existing accounts or register for a new one. This component plays a crucial role in user interaction with your application, handling both logging in and signing up functionalities.

To start with, create a new CSS module. Login.module.css under styles folder. Copy the code from Code 6.7

Code 6.7 – Client -> src -> styles -> Login.module.css

```css
.formContainer {
  max-width: 400px;
  margin: auto;
  text-align: center;
  margin-top: 40px;
}
.inputField {
  margin-bottom: 1rem !important;
}

.btn {
  margin-bottom: 1rem !important;
}
```

Next, create a file named Login.tsx in the components folder. You can use the code provided in Code 6.8. I will go into detail about this code in the following explanation.

Code 6.8 – Client -> src -> components -> Login.tsx

```tsx
import React, { useState, useContext } from 'react';
import { TextField, Button, Typography, Link, Snackbar,
Alert } from '@mui/material';
import styles from '../styles/Login.module.css';
```

```typescript
import { AuthDispatchContext } from './AuthProvider';
import { useNavigate } from 'react-router-dom';

interface User {
  username: string;
  password: string;
  name: string;
  email: string;
  address: string;
}

const Login = () => {
  const setLoggedInUser = useContext(AuthDispatchContext);
  const [isSignUp, setIsSignUp] = useState(false);

const [username, setUsername] = useState('');
  const [password, setPassword] = useState('');
  const [name, setName] = useState('');
  const [email, setEmail] = useState('');
  const [address, setAddress] = useState('');
  const [openSnackbar, setOpenSnackbar] = useState(false);
  const [snackMessage, setSnackMessage] = useState('');
  const [severity, setSeverity] = useState<"success" |
"error" | "info" | "warning" | undefined>("success");
  const navigate = useNavigate();

  const handleCloseSnackbar = () => {
    setOpenSnackbar(false);
    if (severity === "success" && isSignUp) {
      setIsSignUp(!isSignUp);
    }
  }
  const setErrorSnack = (errorMessage: string) => {
    setSnackMessage(errorMessage);
```

```
      setSeverity("error");
      setOpenSnackbar(true);
   }
  const validateFields = () => {
      // Regex to validate email format
      const emailRegex = /^[^\s@]+@[^\s@]+\.[^\s@]+$/;


  if ((!isSignUp && (!username || !password)) || (isSignUp
&& (!username || !password || !name || !email ||
!address))) {
      setSnackMessage("You must fill in all fields");
      setSeverity("error");
      setOpenSnackbar(true);
      return false;
    }
    // Check for valid email if isSignUp is true
    if (isSignUp && !emailRegex.test(email)) {
      setSnackMessage("You must enter a valid email
address");
      setSeverity("error");
      setOpenSnackbar(true);
      return false;
    }
    return true;
  };

  const signUp = () => {
    const newUser: User = {
      username,
      password,
      name,
      email,
      address,
```

```javascript
    };

    // Make a fetch call to the signup endpoint
    fetch('/api/users/signup', {
      method: 'POST',

  headers: {
        'Content-Type': 'application/json',
      },
      body: JSON.stringify(newUser),
    })
      .then(response => {
        if (response.ok) {
          return response.json();
        } else {
          setErrorSnack("Failed to sign up. Try again");
        }
      })
      .then(data => {
        if (data.success) {
          setUsername('');
          setPassword('');
          setSnackMessage(data.success);
          setSeverity("success");
          setOpenSnackbar(true);
        }
        else {
          if (data.error) {
            setErrorSnack(data.error);
          }
          else {
            setErrorSnack("Failed to sign up. Try again");
          }
```

```
      }
    })

.catch(error => {

  setErrorSnack("Failed to sign up. Try again");
      });


  }

  const login = async () => {
    try {
      const response = await fetch('/api/users/login', {
        method: 'POST',
        headers: {
          'Content-Type': 'application/json',
        },
        body: JSON.stringify({ username, password }),
      });
      if (response.status === 401) {
        setErrorSnack("Incorrect username or password");
        return;
      }
      const data = await response.json();
      if (response.ok) {
        // Login successful
        if (setLoggedInUser) {
          setLoggedInUser(data.username);
        }

  navigate("/catalog");
      }
    else {
```

```
      setErrorSnack("Login failed");
          }

  } catch (error) {
      setErrorSnack("Login failed");
    }
  };

  const handleSubmit = (e: React.FormEvent) => {
    e.preventDefault();
    if (!validateFields()) {
      return;
    }
    isSignUp ? signUp() : login()
  };

  const toggleSignUp = () => {
    setIsSignUp(!isSignUp);
  };

  return (
    <div className={styles.formContainer}>
      <Typography variant="h4" gutterBottom>
        {isSignUp ? 'Sign Up' : 'Login'}
      </Typography>
      <form >
        {isSignUp && (
          <>

<TextField
              className={styles.inputField}
              label="Name"
              variant="outlined"
```

```
        fullWidth
                value={name}

        onChange={(e) => setName(e.target.value)}
            required
          />
          <TextField
            className={styles.inputField}
            label="Email"
            variant="outlined"
            fullWidth
            value={email}
            onChange={(e) => setEmail(e.target.value)}
            required
          />
          <TextField
            className={styles.inputField}
            label="Address"
            variant="outlined"
            fullWidth
            value={address}
            onChange={(e) => setAddress(e.target.value)}
            required
          />

    </>
      )}
      <TextField
        className={styles.inputField}
        label="Username"

  variant="outlined"
        fullWidth
```

```jsx
          value={username}

      onChange={(e) => setUsername(e.target.value)}
        required
       />
       <TextField
         className={styles.inputField}
         label="Password"
         type="password"
         variant="outlined"
         fullWidth
         value={password}
         onChange={(e) => setPassword(e.target.value)}
         required
       />
       <Button type="submit" variant="contained"
color="primary" className={styles.btn}
onClick={handleSubmit} fullWidth>
         {isSignUp ? 'Sign Up' : 'Login'}
       </Button>
      </form>

  <Typography variant="body1"
className={styles.inputField}>

 {isSignUp ? 'Already have an account? ' : "Not signed up
yet? "}
       <Link component="button" variant="body1"
onClick={toggleSignUp}>
         {isSignUp ? 'Login now' : 'Sign up now'}
       </Link>
      </Typography>
```

```
    <Snackbar open={openSnackbar} autoHideDuration={3000}
onClose={handleCloseSnackbar}>
        <Alert onClose={handleCloseSnackbar}
severity={severity} variant="filled" >
            {snackMessage}
        </Alert>
    </Snackbar>
  </div>

  );
};

export default Login;
```

Let's break down the code:

Structure and Design: The visual part of the Login component includes text fields where users can enter their personal information. These fields include areas to input the username, password, and if signing up, additional details like their name, email, and address. There's also a button that users can click to either log in or sign up, depending on the mode they are in.

Switching Between Modes: Users can switch between login and signup modes based on their needs. If a user already has an account, they can log in using their existing credentials. If not, they can switch to the signup mode to create a new account. This flexibility improves user experience by accommodating both new and returning users in a single, accessible interface.

<u>Validation and Feedback</u>: Before the application processes the login or signup request, it checks to make sure all the required fields are filled out correctly. For instance, during signup, the component also checks that the email address entered is in the correct format. If there's an issue, such as missing information or an incorrect email format, the component will display an error message using MUI Snackbar. This feedback allows users to correct their inputs and understand what might have gone wrong.

<u>Handling User Data</u>: When a user submits their information, the component communicates with the server using the predefined endpoints. We developed and tested these endpoints during stage 2. If signing up, the data is sent to be stored securely in the database. If logging in, the server checks the provided credentials against stored data.

Upon a successful login attempt, the component updates the application's state to reflect the logged-in user's status. This is achieved through the `setLoggedInUser` function, which is provided by the `AuthDispatchContext`. This action effectively signals across the application that a user session has been established, allowing other components to adjust their behavior based on the presence of an authenticated user.

If the login is successful, the user is then navigated to the catalog of products. This is handled using the `useNavigate` hook from `react-router-dom`. In case of errors during login, such as incorrect credentials, appropriate feedback is provided using the Snackbar.

This component ensures that each user's information is securely managed, and that unauthorized access is prevented, maintaining both security and ease of access.

Before we can view this component in the browser, let's first complete Step 3.3, which involves redefining the routes. This setup is essential for properly integrating and displaying the Login component within our application.

Step 3.3: Enhance Routes, Navigation, and Implement Logout Functionality

In the App.tsx file, you will see that the component is wrapped with <Router>, which is actually BrowserRouter that we've imported from react-router-dom.This setup is intended to manage different paths and navigation within the application. When we implement a log out functionality, we will need to use useNavigate hook to navigate to Login component upon successful logout.

However, when you wrap your components with <BrowserRouter> directly in App.tsx, the useNavigate hook isn't accessible in App.tsx itself. This is because useNavigate must be used within a component that is a child of a <Router> component. The reason for this is that the useNavigate hook relies on the context provided by the <Router> to function, and the context isn't available until the component is rendered within the router.

To fix this, an approach is to move the <BrowserRouter> wrapping to an even higher level in the component hierarchy, that is to the index.tsx file. By doing this, you effectively wrap the entire application, including App.tsx, inside the router context. This change allows every component, including App.tsx, to have access to router features, such as the useNavigate hook.

So, firstly, let's update the index.tsx file to include the <Router> wrapping, which was initially in App.tsx. By moving the router to index.tsx, we ensure that the entire application is under the router's context. Additionally, we should wrap the application with AuthProvider at this level too. This adjustment will enable us to manage the logged-in user state effectively, particularly setting it to empty during a logout directly from the App component. Replace the current index.tsx content with the code provided in Code 6.9 to implement these changes.

```tsx
Code 6.9 - Client -> src -> -> index.tsx
import React from 'react';
import ReactDOM from 'react-dom/client';
import './index.css';
import App from './App';
import reportWebVitals from './reportWebVitals';
import { BrowserRouter as Router } from 'react-router-
dom';
import AuthProvider from "./components/AuthProvider";
const root = ReactDOM.createRoot(
  document.getElementById('root') as HTMLElement
);
root.render(
  <React.StrictMode>
    <Router>
      <AuthProvider>
        <App />
      </AuthProvider>
    </Router>
  </React.StrictMode >
);

reportWebVitals();
```

The only modification made to index.tsx is the addition of imports for BrowserRouter and AuthProvider, followed by wrapping the `App` component within these providers. This adjustment ensures that the entire application is encompassed within the routing and authentication contexts provided by BrowserRouter and AuthProvider, respectively.

Next, Let's look at the updates necessary for the App component:

1) Remove the BrowserRouter Wrapper: Since we've already included the BrowserRouter at the top level in index.tsx, we need to eliminate it from App.tsx to avoid redundancy and potential conflicts.

2) Adjust the Default Navigation: Previously, users were directed to the Catalog component upon accessing the homepage. We'll change this so that users are initially directed to the Login component, ensuring they log in before accessing other parts of the application.

3) Add Logout Functionality: We need to incorporate a Logout button within the application's interface. Along with this, we'll implement the functionality to properly handle user logout, effectively clearing the user session and redirecting them to the Login component.

First, update App.module.css by adding the below classes for Logout button and welcome message.

```css
.btn {
    width: 100px;
    margin-left: 40px !important;
    background-color: #ff474c !important;
}
.welcomeMsg
{
    color: yellow;
    display: flex;
    flex-grow: 1;
}
.btnIcon {
    padding-right: 5px;
}
```

Look at Code 6.10 and use it to replace App.tsx. Let me explain the code in detail below.

Code 6.10 - Client -> src -> -> App.tsx

```tsx
// Importing necessary tools from the react toolbox

import {Routes, Route, NavLink } from 'react-router-dom';
// Importing MUI components for the header UI
import { AppBar, Toolbar, Typography, Container, Button }
from '@mui/material';
import StoreTwoToneIcon from '@mui/icons-
material/StoreTwoTone';

// Importing custom components (Catalog, Item, Trolley)
import Catalog from './components/Catalog';
import Trolley from './components/Trolley';
import MyOrders from './components/MyOrders';
import TrolleyProvider from
"./components/TrolleyProvider";

// Import CSS modules
import appStyles from "./App.module.css";

//Added imports
import Login from './components/Login';
import { useContext } from 'react';
import { useNavigate } from 'react-router-dom';
import Logout from '@mui/icons-material/Logout';
import { AuthContext, AuthDispatchContext } from
"./components/AuthProvider";

function App() {
  const navigate = useNavigate();
  const loggedInUser = useContext(AuthContext);
  const setLoggedInUser = useContext(AuthDispatchContext);
```

```
const handleLogout = async (e: React.FormEvent) => {
  e.preventDefault();
  try {

    const response = await fetch('/api/users/logout', {
      method: 'POST',
      headers: {
        'Content-Type': 'application/json',
      },
    });

    if (response.ok) {
      // Handle successful logout

      if (setLoggedInUser) {
        setLoggedInUser("");
      }
      // Redirect to login page
      navigate('/');
    } else {
      console.error('Failed to logout:');
    }
  } catch (error) {
    // Handle error
    console.error('Failed to logout:', error);
  }
}
return (

  <TrolleyProvider>

<div>
```

```jsx
<AppBar position="static">
  <Toolbar>
    <StoreTwoToneIcon fontSize="large" sx={{
paddingRight: "10px" }} />
    <Typography variant="h6" component="div" sx={{
flexGrow: 1 }}>
      MilaJo
    </Typography>
    {loggedInUser && <>
      <NavLink className={({ isActive }) =>
        `${appStyles.menuLink} ${isActive ?
appStyles.activeLink : ""}`
      } to="/catalog" >
        Home
      </NavLink>
      <NavLink className={({ isActive }) =>
        `${appStyles.menuLink} ${isActive ?
appStyles.activeLink : ""}`
      } to="/trolley">
        Trolley
      </NavLink>
      <NavLink className={({ isActive }) =>
        `${appStyles.menuLink} ${isActive ?
appStyles.activeLink : ""}`
      } to="/myorders" >
        My Orders

      </NavLink> <Button type="submit"
variant="contained" color="primary"
className={appStyles.btn} onClick={handleLogout}>
        <Logout className={appStyles.btnIcon}
/>Logout
      </Button></>
    }
```

```
        </Toolbar>
      </AppBar>
      <Container>
        <Routes>
          <Route path="/" element={<Login />} />
          <Route path="/catalog" element={<Catalog />}
/>
          <Route path="/trolley" element={<Trolley />}
/>
          <Route path="/myorders" element={<MyOrders />}
/>
        </Routes>
      </Container>
    </div>
  </TrolleyProvider>
 );
}

export default App;
```

Let's go over the updates we've implemented in the App component.

Initially, we eliminated the import of BrowserRouter since it's no longer utilized in this component due to its relocation to a higher level in the application. We then incorporated imports from the Login component and the useContext and useNavigate hooks . These hooks are essential for accessing the authentication context provided by AuthProvider and managing navigation post-logout.

We also brought in AuthContext and AuthDispatchContext from the AuthProvider. These contexts are used to access and modify the logged-in user state within the component. Additionally, we included the Logout icon from Material-UI for the logout button.

Within the component function, we defined the constant navigate using `useNavigate` to handle redirections. We initialized constants to retrieve the current logged-in user's state and to update this state, using the respective contexts.

The `handleLogout` function was defined to manage user sign-outs. This function makes a server request to log the user out. Upon a successful response, it clears the logged-in status and redirects the user to the login page using the navigate function. This ensures that users are correctly signed out and prevents access to authenticated pages.

In the rendering logic of the component, we removed the `BrowserRouter` wrapper. We introduced conditional rendering based on the user's authentication status. Logged-in users can see navigation links, a welcome message with username, and a logout button. If not logged in, these elements remain hidden, enhancing both the security and the user experience by restricting access to authenticated-only features.

These modifications ensure the App component is optimized for handling user authentication states effectively and securely within the broader application structure.

Before we proceed to the final step, let's first test the signup and login functionality. Start by opening the Visual Studio Code terminal, navigate to the server folder, and execute the command npm `run build-start`. This command builds the client and starts the server, allowing it to listen for requests.

Once the server is up, open your browser and go to `http://localhost:8080/`. At this point, you should see the site logo along with the login form. There will also be an option to switch to the sign-up form if you don't have an account. Note that the navigation links and the logout button will not be visible since no user is logged in yet.

Go ahead and fill in the details on the signup form and click `Sign up`. You should receive a success message upon successful registration. For a visual reference of what to expect, you can refer to Image 6.6. Steps highlighted in lines and numbers.

Image 6.6 Sign Up

After signing up, you will be automatically redirected to the login form within 3 seconds, or you can manually click the "Login now" link to proceed. Once there, enter the username and password you registered with and click on the "Login" button. A successful login will redirect you to the Catalog page, where you will now see all the navigation links, welcome message with username and the logout button.

Refer to Image 6.7 for my example. In this image, you'll notice the logout button and the welcome message are highlighted, illustrating the changes to the navigation bar compared to its previous appearance.

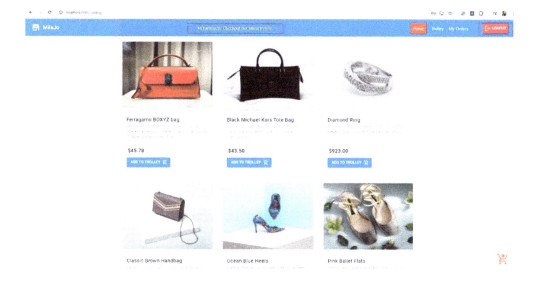

Image 6.7 Logged In

Test the logout functionality to ensure it works as expected. Additionally, you can check the robustness of our login system by attempting to log in with an incorrect username or password, which should result in error messages. Similarly, try signing up again with the same username to confirm that the system appropriately handles duplicate usernames by displaying a "user already exists" message.

Also, you can verify that the signed-up users have been successfully added to your MongoDB user's collection. This step is like how you previously checked the endpoint functionality in the server during Step 2.4. For a visual guide on this verification process, refer to Step 2.4, Image 6.3. This confirmation ensures that our backend is properly recording and storing user data as expected.

With these functionalities confirmed to be working, we are ready to move on to the final step of implementing user-specific trolley and order features. This step is crucial as it personalizes the user experience by linking the shopping cart and order history directly to the logged-in user.

Step 3.4: Revise Trolley and My Orders Components

The final step involves enhancing the Trolley and MOrder components to ensure they handle transactions specific to the logged-in user, moving away from the previous generic approach. This modification not only personalizes the user experience but also boosts security by associating actions directly with authenticated accounts.

Modifications to the Trolley Component (Saving an order)

1) Update Imports: Go to `Trolley.tsx` and begin by adding `import { AuthContext } from "./AuthProvider";` to your Trolley component. This import makes the authentication context available within the Trolley component, allowing it to recognize which user is currently logged in.

2) Accessing the Logged-In User:- Within the Trolley component's function, retrieve the logged-in user's username by adding `const loggedInUser = useContext(AuthContext);`. This line fetches the current user's information from the `AuthContext`, specifically the username, which is vital for personalizing the user's interactions with the cart.

3) Modifying Order Placement Logic:- In the `handlePlaceOrder` function, replace the static assignment `const username = 'globalUser';` with `const username = loggedInUser;`. This change ensures that any orders placed will be attributed to the username of the user who is currently logged in, rather than a generic account.

184

With these changes, the Trolley now operates in a user-specific manner. For instance, if you log in using the username `harireacts` and add items to the Trolley, any orders placed will be recorded under the `harireacts` account. This can be confirmed by checking the `orders` collection in your MongoDB backend, where the order details should reflect this personalized approach.

Modifications to the My Orders Component (Retrieving user specific orders)

1) Update Imports: Start by modifying the import statements at the top of your `MyOrders.tsx` file to include `useContext` from React. This is necessary because you will need to access the user authentication context to identify the logged-in user.

Additionally, add the following line to import the `AuthContext`:

`import { AuthContext } from "./AuthProvider";`

This import makes the authentication context available within the My Orders component, allowing it to recognize which user is currently logged in.

2) Accessing the Logged-In User's Information: Just as you did within the Trolley component, within the function body of the My Orders component, retrieve the logged-in user's username with this line:

`const loggedInUser = useContext(AuthContext);`

This allows the component to fetch the currently logged-in user's username from `AuthContext`.

3) Modifying the Order Retrieval Logic: In the `fetchOrders` function, update the code to fetch orders for the logged-in user instead of a hardcoded user.

Replace the line:
`const response = await fetch(`/api/orders/user/globalUser`);`

With a dynamic fetch request that uses the logged-in user's username:

```
const response = await
fetch(`/api/orders/user/${loggedInUser}`);
```

This modification ensures that the system retrieves orders that belong specifically to the logged-in user, enhancing the personalization of the application and ensuring users only access their own order data. Now the My Orders component is refined to better serve individual users by displaying orders tied specifically to their accounts.

You can test the personalized user experience in your application by following the below steps:

Create Two User Accounts: Start by setting up two distinct user accounts, named userAccount1 and userAccount2.

Testing with userAccount1:

Log In: Sign in using userAccount1.

Browse and Shop: Navigate through the catalog and add a few items to the Trolley.

Place Orders: Complete the checkout process for these items to place multiple orders, Assume that orderA and orderB are the assigned Id's by the system.

View Orders: Navigate to the "My Orders" section to verify that the orders orderA and orderB are correctly listed under this account.

Log Out: Sign out of userAccount1.

Testing with userAccount2:

Log In: Log into the application using userAccount2.

Repeat Shopping Process: Like the first account, browse the catalog, add items to the Trolley, and checkout.

Place Orders: Place a few orders which, for the sake of example, we'll assume are named orderX and orderY by the system.

View Orders: Go to the "My Orders" section. You should see just the orders orderX and orderY, confirming that the orders are user specific.

Log Out: Sign out of userAccount2.

Verify User Isolation:

Re-Log into userAccount1: Sign back into userAccount1 and check the "My Orders" section again. You should only see orderA and orderB, confirming that the orders are isolated per user account and persist correctly across sessions.

This test scenario ensures that each user's interactions are kept private and independent from others, showcasing the effectiveness of our application's user-specific functionalities.

Sip

This chapter covered three pivotal stages in the development of our MERN stack application, each focusing on crucial aspects of user management and authentication. Stage 1 detailed the establishment of a User collection within MongoDB, a foundational step ensuring that user information is securely stored and managed.

Stage 2 shifted our focus to the Node.js environment, where we implemented user-specific routes and integrated Passport.js to authenticate and manage user sessions effectively. This stage was crucial for setting up a secure user registration process and ensuring that order placement and retrieval were gated by user authentication and authorization, thus enhancing the overall security of the application. We also explored the configuration of user authentication routes and the enhancement of session management to safeguard user interactions within the system.

Stage 3 transitioned into React, where we developed and configured a Login component. This component not only supports user authentication but also interacts with the backend to maintain a consistent and secure user registration and login flow. Further refinements included updates to routing and navigation, integrating a logout button to enhance user convenience and security. Additionally, modifications to the Trolley and My Orders components ensured that orders were user-specific, significantly boosting the personalization and security of the application.

By the end of this chapter, we established a comprehensive, user-centric authentication framework within a MERN stack application, illustrating the integration of backend and frontend technologies to create a secure, scalable, and user-friendly online platform.

Note that the final solution is code is available at the GitHub repository, https://github.com/harinvp/merncafe . If you encounter any questions about the material or code detailed in this book, feel free to open an issue in the repository. I am always here to assist and address any concerns you may have.

Last Drop

Throughout this book, we have explored in detail about building robust web applications using the MERN stack, navigating through the aspects of React, MongoDB, Express.js, and Node.js. Starting with the foundational principles of React, we've uncovered the power of its component-based architecture and the efficiency of the Virtual DOM, essential for creating dynamic and responsive user interfaces.

We've integrated TypeScript to enhance code reliability and explored advanced state management techniques with React Context, essential for maintaining a clean and scalable codebase. We expanded on React context for state management, simplifying data sharing across the application without cumbersome prop drilling.

As we delved deeper, combining backend technologies with frontend frameworks felt like blending coffee with milk — effortlessly merging to enhance the overall flavor, much like how client-side and server-side development work together to create a smoother user experience. By implementing features like user authentication and personalized order management, we not only enhanced the application's functionality but also its security, ensuring a safe and user-centric experience.

As we wrap up this fundamental segment of our exploration, we've set the stage for a deeper exploration of the MERN stack's potential. The upcoming parts of this book series will delve into sophisticated React and MERN stack features that were beyond the scope of the initial chapters.

We will refine our codebase by leveraging advanced React hooks such as reducers and custom hooks, enhancing both the cleanliness and efficiency of our code. Further, we'll explore complex topics including rendering optimizations, Server-Side Rendering, (SSR), suspense, and lazy loading to boost the performance and responsiveness of our applications.

Moreover, we'll discuss debugging strategies in React to help identify and resolve issues more efficiently, enhancing the development process. We'll also delve into various design patterns to enrich your grasp of React's application structure and development best practices, along with a preview of the latest features of React 18 to keep you updated on the library's evolution.

On the Node.js front, we will introduce real-time functionalities with WebSocket and investigate microservices architecture to scale and enhance the sophistication of our web projects. We'll address advanced security measures and delve into efficient search mechanisms.

From a database perspective, we'll delve into complex MongoDB concepts such as indexing strategies and data validation rules. We'll explore transactions for handling multi-step tasks and utilize aggregation frameworks for advanced data analysis. Our focus will also extend to optimizing database queries to enhance performance. Additionally, we will cover best practices for data modeling in MongoDB to ensure efficient performance and optimal storage utilization.

Additionally, we will focus on elevating both the design and functionality of our eCommerce site, ensuring it's not just robust but also visually engaging. Discussions on effective hosting solutions for your MERN application will also be included, providing a comprehensive view of deploying and managing your projects.

By the end of this learning, you will not only have a comprehensive mastery of React and the MERN stack but also a professionally designed eCommerce site, showcasing the practical application of your skills and knowledge. This journey will equip you with the tools and insights necessary to create high-performing, scalable, and visually appealing web applications.

Stay caffeinated for more flavorful chapters in our book series!

www.ingramcontent.com/pod-product-compliance
Lightning Source LLC
LaVergne TN
LVHW081342050326
832903LV00024B/1266